A Manual on Task-Switching
or Set-Shifting

Joseph M. Strayhorn
Jillian C. Strayhorn

Psychological Skills Press
Wexford, PA

Published by Psychological Skills Press
www.psyskills.com
Wexford, PA

Author's email: joestrayhorn@gmail.com

ISBN: 978-1-931773-13-3

Contents

Task-Switching: What and Why?

1. This manual is about an activity called task-switching (also known as set-shifting). In task-switching, you have two or more different sets of directions that you can use with the same sorts of situations or problems. You switch back and forth between the different directions. Here's an example of how you can use different directions with the same problem. Look at this math problem:

1. 3+4

One task might be simply to say the answer to the addition question. You'd look at the above stimulus and say "7." But a different task is to say the question and the answer. If this were the task, you'd look at the stimulus above and say, "3+4=7." A third task might be to say the problem number and the answer, in which you'd say "1, 7." So with the same problem, you can follow different directions, or do different tasks.

What is the purpose of this first section?

A. to define and give some examples of set-shifting or task-switching, or
B. to explain why task-switching is a good thing to practice?

2. Another word for the problem or the information you respond to, by following some directions, is a *stimulus*. A math problem was the stimulus in the first example. Here's another example of a stimulus that you can respond to with different tasks. Suppose someone shows you the word *blue*, but it is printed in a different color, such as green (please see the words on the cover of this book). If the task is "read the word," you would say "blue." If the task is "Say what color the word is," you would say "green." So you would respond differently, depending on what the task is. There have been many variations on this activity, which has been called the Stroop task.

The main point of this section is that

A. the Stroop task, another task-switching activity, asks you to either read a word or say what color it is, or
B. the Stroop test is something that is very difficult for some people with concentration problems?

3. Here's another stimulus:

1. fern

It's just a number, followed by a word. One possible set of directions is, "Ignore the number and just read the word." A second possible task is, "Say the sounds of the word separately and then say the word: like "fuh-er-nuh, fern." Saying each of the sounds and then the word is called "sounding and blending." A third possible task is to say the number and then read the word: "1, fern." A fourth task is to say the separate sounds only, without blending, like this: "fuh er nuh." This direction is called "sounds only." With different directions like these, we can use numbered lists of words to practice task-switching at the same time that we are practicing reading.

The purpose of this section was to show how

A. we can practice task-switching with lists of words that we practice reading, as well as with lists of math fact problems,
or
B. saying the sounds of words separately develops a skill called phonemic awareness, that helps people read better?

4. Some research suggests that people with concentration problems find task-switching especially difficult. Some research shows that giving people the medicine that is often given for concentration problems, tends to improve task-switching ability. But research also suggests that lots of practice in task-switching also improves task-switching ability.

Could it be that lots of practice in task-switching would stimulate the growth of the part of the brain that gives us good concentration, impulse control, and decision-making abilities? It's too early to say that this is proved. But practice does tend to improve most skills, and skill improvement happens by the brain's changing in some way.

This section brings up the possibility that

A. people can inherit a certain amount of task-switching ability,
or
B. lots of practice in task-switching could improve concentration, impulse control, and decision-making?

5. How do you do task-switching well? Let's imagine that you can hold in your mind only so much information at any one time, and let's call the amount of information you can hold, your "working memory." To do tasks such as addition facts takes a certain amount of working memory. But to do task switching, you have to devote some of your working memory to remembering what you are supposed to be doing – what the directions are. Thus dividing your working memory between doing something and remembering what you are supposed to do is part of the art of task switching.

The point of this section is that

A. no one knows how much practice in task switching is enough to have positive effects,
or
B. good task switching requires using some of your working memory to do something, and some of it to remember what you're supposed to do?

6. Do we ever need to do task-switching in real life? In school work, task switching is very frequently useful. Here's a stimulus you might get in grammar class:

I don't got any fruit.

The sentence should read, I don't have any fruit. But what is the task? It could be lots of different things. The teacher's directions could be, "Draw a circle around the error." Or they could be, "Draw one line through the error and write the correct word right over it." Or they could be, "Rewrite the sentence correctly, on this paper, just below the sentence." Or they could be, "Write the sentence correctly on you own paper." It happens very frequently that kids look at their schoolwork and don't follow the directions. And this particularly is a problem for students that people say have "attention problems," or "attention deficit disorder."

This section

A. promises that by task-switching you can solve attention problems,
or
B. gives an example of a real-life situation in school where good task-switching is an important ability to have?

7. Here's another example. The stimulus is that a bunch of your classmates are near you. If the situation is that you're outside sitting in a park having lunch, the task might be to talk and joke around and have as much fun as you can. If you're sitting in the classroom working on an in-class assignment or test, the task might be to ignore your classmates and say nothing to them. Again, the two stimuli are similar, but the tasks are very different. Kids with "attention deficit disorder" tend to have problems task-switching in this way, but almost all other kids also are challenged by it too.

This section made the point that

A. knowing when the talk and joke with classmates and when to ignore them is a task-switching activity,
or
B. it's not just for the teacher, but for the student's benefit, to be quiet in a classroom during a test?

8. Here's another example. This time, imagine that the stimulus for a student is the student's room, which contains various things including school books

and electronic toys. At certain times, the "directions" the student gives himself or herself are, "Ignore the electronic toys, and do the homework." At other times, the "directions" are, "ignore the schoolbooks and enjoy the electronic toys." Again, the job is to respond to the same stimulus in different ways, depending on what the directions are at a certain time. There's a need to hold in memory, "Here's what I'm supposed to be doing now," while using the rest of your working memory to do it.

This section makes the point that

A. people with attention deficit disorder often find it hard to ignore the temptation of electronic toys,
or
B. following the "directions" one gives oneself to work or play while in one's room is a task-switching activity?

9. Here's another example. Someone plays a bunch of videogames where the best strategy is to react as quickly as possible as soon as a new situation comes up. Then the person plays a chess game on the computer, where the best strategy is to take the time to make very careful plans before reacting to any new situation. The stimuli in the two situations are similar (both appear on screens) but not exactly the same. It's necessary to do task-switching to move from the directions of "react as quickly as you can" to the directions of "react only after making very careful plans."

This section made the point that

A. chess is better than most other videogames,
or
B. switching between "react fast" and "react with careful planning" strategies is another type of task-switching?

10. Switching between "react fast" and "react after taking your time to decide carefully" of course goes on not just with videogames and computer games, but in countless life situations. If I'm driving and a kid on a bike rides out in front of me, I'm definitely in the "react fast" situation. If I'm thinking of getting married to someone, I'm definitely in the "react only after taking time to decide carefully" situation.

Both of the "stimuli" we've just mentioned are somewhat similar, in that they are "choice points" – situations where I have to decide what to do. But the directions one should give oneself on how fast to make the decision are drastically different.

This section makes the point that

A. in life, it's necessary to do a lot of task-switching to decide when to use the "react fast" strategy and when to use the "take your time to decide carefully" strategy,
or

B. whom you get married to is a decision that will affect the rest of your life?

11. Here's another example of how there are two types of "directions" to follow, in situations that are somewhat similar. The situation is that of "a choice point involving danger"; the two types of directions are "be brave and take a big risk," or "take care of yourself and don't take a risk."

Suppose that the danger is that there's a burning house, and a child trapped inside. A firefighter decides to take a risk and go inside to rescue the child. The firefighter is successful, and people greatly admire the firefighter for courage.

Now suppose the firefighter gets invited by a friend to go rock-climbing. The idea this friend has is that you climb straight up a cliff, without using a rope to catch yourself if you should fall. The firefighter looks at the situation and tells the friend, "No way."

The firefighter has done some task-switching here. In both situations, the stimulus is a choice point; in the first, the task was to overcome fear and be brave; in the second, the task was to listen to realistic fear and be cautious.

The story described in this section involved task-switching because

A. the firefighter had to have lots of courage to rescue the child,
or

B. the firefighter responded to the situation of "a choice point involving danger" using two different sets of directions?

12. I could give you lots of other examples where task-switching is very important in real life. Does doing lots of task switching practice with things like lists of math fact problems or reading words increase your ability to do task-switching in real life? It's too soon to answer that question for sure, but this is our hope. Even if this hope doesn't come true, doing lots of task-switching practice with math facts and reading words will at the very least probably get you lots better at doing math facts and reading words! And these are very important skills for success at school. So even if the task-switching skill you practice doesn't carry over, or generalize, to real life, you will not have wasted your time by practicing.

This section makes the point that

A. we know for sure that practicing task-switching with math facts will help you in all other types of task-switching, or
B. practicing task-switching with math facts will at the very least help you with math facts, and this is a great skill for success in school?

13. There's some evidence that task-switching activities of many different types all call for the activity of a certain

part of the brain, near the front of the head, called the prefrontal cortex. There's also some evidence that when we do lots of activities that use a certain part of the brain, that part gets better and better at what it does, as if it is strengthened. Probably something like this happens each time we get better and better at any skill by practicing it. It's probably too simple to say that practicing a lot of task-switching grows or strengthens your prefrontal cortex. But it wouldn't be at all unusual to find that practicing concentration and intense mental activity helped people to get better at similar mental activities. There's some evidence in the research that practicing certain task-switching activities makes improvements in the brain so that other task-switching activities also become easier.

The author in this section states that some evidence leads us to believe that

A. practicing math facts will help you even in advanced math,
or
B. practicing task-switching activities will help you in other task-switching activities?

14. How do you practice task-switching? Some people are trying to make up video games that will be entertaining, and at the same time will give practice in task-switching. It could be that this strategy will be successful.

But this book uses a different strategy. It's our prediction that you have to practice task-switching for many, many hours before your brain grows more competent at task-switching. One of the big ideas of this book is the following: why not practice task-switching at the same time that you are teaching yourself other things that are useful to know?

Two of the main things people need to spend a long time working at, while in school, are learning math facts and learning to read words. This book gives you lists of math facts and reading words, and asks you to task switch back and forth between two different sets of directions on how to practice them.

The main point of this section is that

A. it's possible to practice task-switching with physical activities,
or
B. this book gives you task-switching activities that also give you practice in math facts and reading words?

15. Suppose you see the following stimulus:

1. 2+6

We'll use four different ways that you can respond. If the directions are "Answer only," or "A only," then you just respond by saying, "8." If the directions are "Question and Answer," or "Q and A," then you respond by saying "2+6=8." If the directions are "Number and answer," or "Num and A," then you respond by saying "1, 8." If the directions are "Sum-1st=2nd," then you would say "8-2=6." In other words, for Sum-1st=2nd, you first add the numbers, and then say that the sum minus the first number equals the second number.

If you see the following stimulus,

4. 3x7

Then for "A only" you'd say 21, for Q+A you'd say "3 times 7 = 21," for Num and A you'd say "4, 21." For "Product divided by first = second," which we'll abbreviate "P/1st=2nd," you'd say "21 divided by 3=7."

With these four sets of directions, you can practice a lot of task switching as you are practicing math facts.

The purpose of this section was

A. to explain the different types of directions used when you task-switch while practicing math facts,
or
B. to explain why lots of skill with math facts will come in handy?

16. Now suppose you see a numbered list of reading words, like this:

1. ban
2. cat

3. fax

If the directions are "sound and blend," or S and B, you say "buh-aah-nnuh ban, cuh aah tuh cat, fuh aah ks fax." If the directions are "blend only," or B only, you just say "ban, cat, fax." If the directions are "Number and blend," or "Num and B," you would say "1, ban; 2, cat; 3, fax." If the directions are "sound only," or "S only," you would say "buh aah nnuh, cuh aah tuh, fuh aah ks."

When you get to longer words, you will sound and blend by syllable. For example, suppose you see

1. en ter tain ing entertaining

If the directions are "sound and blend," (S and B) you would say "en ter tain ing entertaining." If the directions are "blend only" (B only), you would say "entertaining." If the directions are "number and blend" (Num and B), you would say "1, entertaining." If the directions are "sound only" (S only) you would say "en ter tain ing."

We are repeating ourselves sometimes in summarizing these directions; that's because they are important to understand if this book is to be useful.

The main purpose of this section was to

A. explain why sounding and blending by syllables is better for longer words,

or
B. explain the different types of directions used with reading words?

17. We also have some math word problems for you to practice with. We'll use two types of directions for these. Suppose the stimulus is:

1. Jay types 2 pages, and then 3 more. How many has he typed in all?

If the directions are "A only," you say the answer to the problem – you'd just say "5." If the directions are "Which operation," which we'll abbreviate "Which Op," you say whether you add, subtract, multiply, or divide to get the answer. So for the word problem above, you'd say "Add."

For the word problems you'll see later on, are there

A. 4 types of directions,
or
B. 2 types of directions?

18. If you can learn to do math facts quickly and automatically, without having to think about them, you're going to find that the rest of your math career is lots easier than it would otherwise be. Even on tests of advanced math, it's great to be able to do the four basic operations quickly and easily. Some people think, "I'll just do calculations on a calculator." But having to pull out a calculator every time you want to combine two numbers slows you way down. Learning to do the math facts really quickly is a great thing to do.

Likewise, learning to be able to call out just about any word, with a reasonable guess at how it's pronounced, is a great skill also. You'll be much more able to figure out new words from reading them, if you can pronounce them to yourself. Learning to read words fluently is one of the most important skills for anyone's education. If you already can read very fluently, learning to "sound and blend" will help you greatly if you teach someone else to read!

This section is

A. a sales pitch on why skills in math facts and word-reading are very useful for you,
or
B. a sales pitch on why task-switching is important for you?

19. As you practice task-switching with math facts or reading or anything else, it's important to use what we call good "hierarchy-ology." This means arranging it so that the tasks you do are at the right point on the "hierarchy of difficulty." The hierarchy of difficulty is a usually imaginary list of challenges, starting from very easy ones and going up to very hard ones. If you are trying things that are too easy, you'll usually feel bored. If you are trying things that

are too hard, you'll usually feel frustrated. If you're at just the right level of challenge, you'll find the activity much more pleasant.

The main point of this section is that

A. you want your task-switching practice sessions to be not too hard, not too easy, but just at the right level of difficulty,
or
B. you need lots of self-discipline to keep practicing task-switching?

20. When you are doing math facts, task-switching adds more difficulty to a task that can be already difficult. So here's a very important recommendation. For any page of math facts, first practice just looking at the questions and saying the answers, without worrying about the directions. When you get familiar enough with the math facts that you can do them all correctly, fairly rapidly (about 30 per minute) then add the task-switching and keep practicing. Keep going until you can do the facts with the task-switching, about as fast as you can get the words out of your mouth.

The author recommends

A. doing task-switching from the very start with any given page of math facts,
or

B. first practicing the math facts without task-switching, then adding the task-switching?

21. The same goes for reading words. If you are finding it very difficult just to read the words, adding task switching can make the whole task too frustrating. Work on the list of words until you can comfortably read them correctly, then go back and work on task switching.

The additional work that you do, after you have already learned to do the page fairly comfortably, is where you really get tremendous benefit. Most people don't realize this, and stop drilling when they are "fairly OK" at doing something rather than keeping on until they are "totally proficient" in it.

The author feels that

A. when you can do a page with all items correct, it's time to go on,
or
B. when you can do a page with all items correct, that's when your additional work will yield you the most benefit?

22. We recommend the following procedure once you start task-switching: for any given page of problems or words, there are two types of directions. For example, "Q and A" or "A only." First, go through the entire page using the first way of answering the questions, and time yourself. Then go through the page again, using the

second way of answering the questions, and time yourself. One of these ways will almost always be slower. For example, you have a lot more to say when you do "Q and A" than when you do "A only." But the average of the two speeds gives you an estimate of how fast you could go doing half one way and half the other way. Then you time yourself again, this time doing the task-switching. The difference between the average that you computed and the time for task-switching is the "cost" for task-switching. The closer you can get this difference to zero, the more you are doing the task-switching quickly and automatically.

The "cost" of task-switching represents

A. how difficult the math facts are,
or
B. how much longer it takes you to do the challenge with switching than without?

23. Task-switching is an important skill because it's a member of a very important set of skills called *executive functions*. These are the skills involved in thinking about what you want in the future, working for future gain and not just short-term pleasure, planning, making good decisions, and keeping on track with what you're supposed to be doing. Someone who is very skilled in executive functions is much more likely to be successful in all areas of life. Task-switching may be a great way to

build up the "mental muscles" that are involved in executive functioning, particularly the part having to do with "keeping on track with what you're supposed to be doing."

The point of this section is that

A. task-switching is one of a set of important skills called executive functioning skills, that involve making good plans and carrying them out,
or
B. task-switching requires lots of mental effort?

24. There's another benefit of doing the exercises in this book: an increase in "work capacity." It takes a lot of mental effort just to practice math facts and read lists of words. It takes even more concentration and mental effort when you add task-switching to the challenge! Some people get tired of putting out mental effort very quickly – they have lower "work capacity" than the people who can keep on doing mental work for a long time. Having lots of work capacity lets you finish more of the things you need to do to accomplish your goals. It's a very important skill to have.

You increase your physical work capacity by doing lots of exercise. People who train and push their bodies to improve can do enormously much more physical work than those who do not train. Part of the idea of this book is that you can increase your mental work capacity by lots of training and practice, very much like physical work capacity.

The main idea of this section is that

A. by training and doing mental workouts, you can increase your ability to tolerate lots of mental work, or
B. it does little good to have high work capacity if you're doing the wrong task?

25. If you are either the tutor or the student who is getting ready to lead or do the exercises in this book, it will help you very much if you can convince yourself that

1. task-switching
2. work capacity
3. math facts (and word problems)
4. and word-reading

are all very important skills, and that they are worth a great deal of work to improve.

The main point of this section is that

A. the lists to follow will task-switch between two different directions, or
B. it will be easier to do the exercises that follow if you're convinced that the skills they exercise are important ones for you?

26. You'll probably also be more successful if you expect, and are not

scared of, some fatigue. When people work out physically, they get very tired. But they don't mind getting tired, because they know they are increasing their strength and endurance. If you can have the same attitude toward mental fatigue, that will help you greatly. It will help if you can think, "I'm tired, but that's good! That means I'm probably improving my work capacity!" The more you can think this instead of "I'm tired – that means I must stop!" the better you'll do.

This section is promoting

A. an attitude toward mental fatigue that says, "This means I'm improving," rather than "This means I need to stop," or
B. the idea that you should do lots of physical exercise as well as mental exercise?

27. Just as when you are getting into good physical shape, you want to take it gradually. Someone who wants to someday run a marathon does not try to run 26 miles on the first day of training. It's best to start with a challenge that will make you push yourself some, but not one that will be very painful for you. You give yourself time to build up your endurance. The same thing goes for mental work. When starting out, 5 minutes of work per day on task-switching may be plenty. After training, one can work up to a good deal more than that.

The main idea is that

A. people are different from the very start in how much work capacity they have,
or
B. it's good to start out with a little task-switching and gradually build up your "mental muscles" to the point where you're doing lots more?

28. This sort of training is like training for a race in another way, too. You don't just do the exercises. You do them and time yourself, and you get yourself very motivated to improve your speed. You compare your speeds to your previous speeds. You don't do any given page just once. If it's worth doing, it's worth doing several times, to see if you can get faster and faster. If you do get much faster by practicing, you try to really celebrate that, and to feel just great about it.

A summary of this section is that

A. you have lots of work to do if you want to get really good at the skills this book helps you practice,
or
B. you don't just do the work, but measure how fast you can do it, and greatly celebrate when you improve your speed?

29. Especially when you're starting out, it's good to do task-switching in some

ways that don't get you quite as tired as doing math facts or reading word lists. So before we go into practicing task-switching while doing math and reading, let's mention, in the next chapter, some games and activities that also let you practice task-switching.

The next chapter will describe

A. games and activities for task switching,
or
B. math and reading activities?

Some Task-Switching Games

Beach Ball Throwing

30. There are several ways to throw a beach ball with two hands, but two of them are "overhand" and "underhand." When you throw it overhand, your fingers point up; when you throw it underhand, your fingers point down. The first activity is called "Same." This means that when the tutor throws the ball overhand, the student throws it back overhand; when the tutor throws the ball underhand, the student throws it back underhand.

   Then at some point, the tutor calls out, "other." From now until when the tutor says "Same" again, the student throws the ball back in the other way from the way the tutor threw it. That is, when the tutor throws it overhand, the student throws it back underhand, and vice versa.

   The tutor and the student can switch roles, so that the student gets to call whether the directions are "same" or "other."

The better summary of this task-switching activity is that

A. the directions alternate between "throw it back the same way I throw it" and "throw it back the other way,"

or
B. the tutor and student throw the ball back and forth a lot?

Jumping Jacks, and other varieties of Two Motions

31. The exercise called "jumping jacks" has two parts. In one, you move your hands from down at your sides, out, up to over your head. In the second, you jump your feet from a "together" position to a "spread apart" position.

   In this activity, you'll be doing one of those parts at a time. When the directions are "same," the tutor does either the hands part or the legs part, and the student does the same thing. When the tutor says "other," the student works the legs whenever the tutor works the arms, and the student works the arms whenever the tutor works the legs.

The better summary of this activity is that

A. it's good to do some jumping when you're restless,
or
B. you alternate between two conditions, one where the student does the same exercise as the tutor, and one where the student does the other one?

32. You can make up an unlimited number of variations on this, all of which can be called "Two Motions." You define any two ways of exercising, moving, or wiggling. One variation is "runs and squats," where the two tasks are running in place and doing knee bends. Another is "curls and presses," where both tutor and student have some dumbbells in hand, and the two tasks are doing curls (using your biceps to lift the weight from waist to shoulder) and doing presses (using your shoulder muscles to lift the weight from shoulder to fully extended overhead).

To make this activity more fun, invent a new type of funny wiggle every time you do it. Get the student involved in making up the two movements to do. Let the student be the "caller" of "same" or "other," some of the time. Do it to music if you want.

This is a good way to practice task-switching when the student has been sitting down reading and doing math for long enough to get restless!

The author seems to hope that the "two motions" activity can be done

A. in a gleeful way,
or
B. in a very serious way?

Tick Tock

33. As in the first two activities, there is a "same" direction and an "other"

direction. You decide on two words – tick and tock, for this example, but they could be "Bye" and "Hi," or "Up" and "Down," or "Snake" and "Grape," or whatever you want. If the directions are "same," then the student says whatever word the tutor said, right after the tutor says it. If the directions are "other," the student says the other word. So a round could start like this:

Tutor: Same! tick
Student: tick
Tutor: tick
Student: tick
Tutor: tock
Student: tock
Tutor: Other! tock
Student: tick
Tutor: tick
Student: tock

One of the advantages of this activity is that you can do it over the phone.

The two different tasks that make this a task switching activity are

A. saying tick or saying tock,
or
B. saying the same word the tutor said, or the other word?

Regular Simon Says and Reverse Simon Says

34. The regular version of the game Simon Says goes like this: the leader

says to do a bunch of things. If the leader says "Simon says jump up and down," you're supposed to jump up and down. If the leader says "Jump up and down," you're *not* supposed to jump up and down. That is, you only obey Simon, not just generic commands.

In Reverse Simon Says, the directions are the opposite. If the leader says "Say *house*," you say *house*; if the leader says "Simon says say *frog*," you don't say *frog*.

So in this activity, the tutor calls out "regular!" and "reverse" to signal which set of directions applies. Or if you want, the directions can be "Obey Simon" and "Disobey Simon."

If you stuck to commands like saying words, humming, whistling, yawning loudly, sneezing, coughing, and other things that you can hear, would it be possible to do this game over the phone?

A. yes,
or
B. no?

Alternate Reading

35. A major activity we have used in psychoeducational tutoring is alternate reading – the tutor and the student take turns reading aloud to each other. In a book like this, we have usually taken turns by the numbered section: for example, if the tutor reads section 24, the student would read section 25.

To make alternate reading a task-switching activity, you can switch among different ways of alternating. You can take turns every sentence or every paragraph, and switch back and forth between these two.

Switching between alternating by sentence and alternating by paragraph is a task-switching activity because

A. you have to hold in mind the directions of when to give the other person a turn, as well as holding in mind whatever you are reading,
or
B. taking turns reading makes a social activity out of something that would otherwise be done alone?

Typing Lessons

36. The student puts fingers on the home keys, in the standard position for touch typing. That is: left little finger on a, left ring on s, left middle on d, left index on f. Right index on j, right middle on k, right ring on l, and right little on semicolon. The right thumb depresses the space bar.

The first task, "letter only," is that when the tutor calls out a letter on the home row, the student types the letter (with the correct finger!) These letters can include g and h, which are typed with the left index and right index respectively. After typing them, the student returns the fingers to the home keys. If the tutor calls out "space," the student presses the space bar with the right thumb.

The second task, "diagonal," is that when the tutor calls out a letter, the student types the "diagonal" that is typed with the same finger that is used to type that letter. Thus when the tutor calls out "a," the student types "aqaz" followed by a space. When the tutor calls out "s," the response is swsx, and so on, for dedc, frfv, gtgb, hyhn, jujm, kik, lol., and ;p;/.

The tutor switches back and forth between these two tasks by calling out "letter only" and "diagonal."

If the student practices task-switching with these two activities enough, the student is well on the way to learning touch typing.

The alternation just described in this activity is

A. between typing a letter on the home row and typing the diagonal that goes with that letter,
or
B. typing a space after the letter or not typing a space after the letter?

37. Here's another similar typing activity. This one takes the student up the hierarchy of typing skill after mastering the previous activity.

The tutor calls out any letter of the alphabet, or semicolon, slash, comma, or period. In the first task, called "diagonal," the job of the student is to type (with the correct finger!) the diagonal that contains that letter or punctuation mark. For example, if the tutor calls out "c," the student types dedc followed by a space. If the tutor calls out "comma," the student types kik, followed by a space.

The second task is "letter only." Now if the tutor calls out "c," the student types the letter c, using the left middle finger. The tutor alternates between "letter only" and "diagonal," as before.

In this activity, the tutor can call out letter sequences that make words. If the sequences make words even during the "diagonal" part of the activity, the resulting diagonals make a secret code of sorts.

The words the tutor uses to switch tasks in this exercise are

A. the same as in the previous typing exercise,
or
B. are different from in the previous typing exercise?

Stroop Number

38. This activity is a way to do a version of a Stroop test. There are two sets of directions: Repeat the Number and Count the Numbers.

The tutor says the number one, two, three, or four, and says it either one, two, three, or four times. If the directions are "Repeat the number," or just "Repeat!" you just repeat whatever number the tutor said. If the directions are "Count the numbers," or just "Count!" you count how many times the tutor said the number and say the number you get from counting.

So here's an example:

Tutor: Repeat! 3, 3.
Student: 3.
Tutor: 1, 1, 1, 1.
Student: 1.
Tutor: Count! 1, 1.
Student: 2
Tutor: 3, 3, 3, 3.
Student: 4.

Should it be possible to do this activity over the phone?

A. yes,
or
B. no?

Subset and Superset

39. The tutor says a word like "dog." If the directions are "subset," then you say a subset of dogs – like "collie" or "beagle." If the directions are "superset," then you say a class of which dogs are a subset – for example, "animals" or "mammals." The directions alternate, as in the other activities.

Here's an example:

Tutor: Subset! Clothing.
Student: Shirt.
Tutor: Machine.

Student: Computer.
Tutor: Silverware.
Student: Fork.
Tutor: Superset! Pencil.
Student: School supplies.
Tutor: Nickel.
Student: Coins.
Tutor: Guitar.
Student: Musical instruments.

Which of the following is correct?

A. vegetables is a subset of foods,
or
B. vegetables is a superset of foods?

Singing in Harmony and Unison

40. As long as we'll be working on math facts, here's a way to work on them that will appeal to those who are musically inclined. I've written some skip-counting songs to help people learn multiplication. For example, the lyrics to one of these songs is

3, 6, 9, 12, 15, 18
21, 24, 27, 30.

There is a regular melody for this, and a harmony part. You can sing the two parts in harmony, and it sounds good. I hope that you can find these melodies on the internet, by the time you read this.

Singing harmony is sort of a task-switching activity in itself, because you have to alternate in your mind between listening to the other person's note and listening to your own note.

What makes this an even greater task switching activity is this. One person just sings the melody. The other person, the task-switcher, shifts back and forth between singing the harmony part and singing in unison with the other singer. This is hard enough that the task switcher should be able to decide upon his or her own time to switch.

Of course, any other song with two part harmony is also one you can use for this activity.

A task-switching part of this activity is

A. following the different directions of "sing in unison" or "sing in harmony," or
B. remembering the skip counting numbers, if you are using a skip-counting song?

Practicing Task-Switching with Math Facts

Our philosophy with this book is that task-switching may turn out to be a great way of "building up" extremely useful portions of the prefrontal cortex or other brain regions that help with "executive functioning," or delaying gratification, planning, and decision-making. But at this point, no one knows how many hours of task-switching practice are sufficient to produce maximum benefit. But if you can practice task-switching at the same time that you practice academic skills that are crucial to your success in school, you are practicing two very important things at once. If task-switching practice turns out to be less useful than we predict, you still will not have wasted your time, because you will have practiced academic skills.

The two skills that take up most of the pages that follow are math facts and word-reading. The student who can not only do these "well enough," but who can do them totally fluently and automatically, has a major advantage in all future school work.

Let's talk first about the math facts pages.

The first task with any of these pages is to get to the point where you can say the answers correctly. Once you can do that, then you go for greater and greater speed. Any time trial can be done in either of two ways: you time how long it takes to do all 100 problems, or you time and see how many problems you can do in one minute.

Let's review the way to calculate the "cost" of task-switching. You ignore the written directions and have a time trial with one of the directions. Then you have another time trial, using the other directions. You average those two times. Then, you do a time trial with the switching in effect. (If you make an error, including the error of following the wrong directions, the tutor corrects the error and the student goes back and says the item correctly. Thus making errors adds to the time for the time trial.)

You find the difference between speed with switching and speed without switching. The answer is the cost of switching. As you get better and better at task-switching, that cost will go down and down.

Periodically, you can ignore the directions and just say the answers to the math facts. You should shoot for over 60 answers per minute, all correct.

The addition facts go through a certain sequence. We start with the plus 0's, plus 1's, and plus 2's, which are easy to do by counting up. Then we do the plus 10's, which are easy to do by adding a one before the number to be added to 10. Then we do the doubles, such as 6+6, which are easy for most people to remember. Next comes the "one aparts," such as 6+7. You can figure these out from knowing the doubles – if 6+6 is 12, then 6+7 is one more than 12, or 13. Next come the "two aparts," which also can be figured out from the doubles. In figuring out 6+8, for example, you can take one off the 8 and put it on the 6, and realize that the answer is the same as 7+7, or 14. Then we do the plus 9's, which are one less than the corresponding plus 10. Finally, there are 6 more facts that don't yield to any of the tricks above, that can be figured out in any of several other ways.

Please don't hesitate to do any given page of facts several times. Keep a record of the speed with which the task was done, and see how much the speed can increase. It is a very good idea to graph, or at least put into a table, the speed for any page, over repeated trials. If at all possible, the student should become very involved in recording and graphing the speeds and in celebrating new speed records. If the student finds the task so hard as to be very frustrating, practice it more without task-switching or go back to an easier page.

Addition Facts

Plus 0's, Plus 1's, and Plus 2's.

For "A only," (that is, "Answer only") When you see 2+7, say 9. For "Q and A," (or "Question and Answer") when you see 2+7, say "2+7=9."

Q and A
1. 0+9
2. 2+4
3. 1+5
4. 1+7
5. 3+2
6. 10+1
7. 9+2
8. 8+0
9. 1+6
10. 2+7
A only
11. 1+8
12. 2+7
13. 8+1
14. 10+1
15. 8+0
16. 3+0
17. 2+9
18. 8+1
Q and A
19. 5+1
20. 7+1
21. 1+10
22. 3+0
23. 2+8
24. 4+0
25. 1+0
26. 1+10
27. 5+2
A only
28. 1+1

29. 9+1
30. 0+10
31. 0+9
32. 9+2
33. 0+0
34. 2+3
35. 1+5
36. 1+7
37. 1+9
Q and A
38. 6+0
39. 5+0
40. 3+1
41. 3+2
42. 6+2
43. 3+0
44. 10+1
45. 0+6
A only
46. 0+10
47. 4+1
48. 1+8
49. 6+0
50. 10+1
51. 10+1
52. 0+0
53. 9+1
54. 9+1
Q and A
55. 0+2
56. 7+1
57. 7+1

58. 1+4
59. 10+0
60. 3+1
61. 6+2
62. 3+1
63. 3+2
64. 2+2
65. 6+2
A only
66. 8+2
67. 2+8
68. 2+8
69. 9+1
70. 0+5
71. 6+0
72. 2+0
73. 4+1
74. 3+1
Q and A
75. 10+2
76. 2+0
77. 1+6
78. 3+2
79. 2+8
80. 10+2
81. 1+9
82. 1+3
83. 10+2
84. 0+3
85. 5+1
A only
86. 2+4

87. 1+5
88. 0+6
89. 0+9
90. 6+1
91. 10+2
92. 0+5
93. 0+2
94. 1+8
95. 1+4
96. 4+1
97. 0+6
98. 5+2
99. 1+1
Q and A
100. 2+7

Plus 0's, Plus 1's, and Plus 2's, Set 2

For "Num and A," (or "Number and Answer") when you see 1. 2+7, say "1, 9."

A only
1. 2+7
2. 10+0
3. 0+8
4. 1+7
5. 2+2
6. 8+0
7. 5+1
8. 6+0
9. 1+1
10. 2+7
11. 2+8
Num and A
12. 1+8
13. 4+1
14. 1+9
15. 6+1
16. 2+7
17. 0+8
18. 5+2
19. 1+9
20. 0+0
21. 0+6
A only
22. 1+4
23. 1+10
24. 2+7
25. 0+9
26. 2+1
27. 5+2
Num and A
28. 4+0
29. 0+4
30. 5+2

31. 6+2
32. 0+7
33. 0+0
34. 1+9
35. 9+1
36. 0+5
A only
37. 3+0
38. 3+0
39. 0+6
40. 9+0
41. 2+7
42. 1+9
43. 9+0
Num and A
44. 1+0
45. 1+7
46. 7+2
47. 0+6
48. 5+1
49. 0+8
50. 1+6
51. 0+1
52. 5+2
53. 1+5
A only
54. 10+2
55. 4+2
56. 8+2
57. 2+0
58. 2+5
59. 7+1
60. 4+1
61. 3+1

62. 1+3
Num and A
63. 0+0
64. 1+9
65. 1+1
66. 0+6
67. 7+2
68. 9+1
69. 1+9
70. 7+2
A only
71. 10+1
72. 1+2
73. 0+3
74. 5+1
75. 1+3
76. 4+2
77. 2+9
78. 0+8
79. 2+3
80. 1+9
Num and A
81. 2+5
82. 0+8
83. 7+1
84. 2+3
85. 1+4
86. 8+0
87. 1+4
88. 9+0
89. 5+2
90. 0+4
A only
91. 1+6

92. 5+0
93. 4+2
94. 10+1
95. 5+0
96. 10+2
Num and A
97. 2+2
98. 0+4
99. 8+0
100. 0+2

Plus 10's, Set 1

Q and A
1. 10+9
2. 10+8
3. 10+6
4. 10+4
5. 3+10
6. 10+3
7. 10+8
8. 0+10
A only
9. 10+0
10. 7+10
11. 7+10
12. 6+10
13. 6+10
14. 1+10
15. 9+10
16. 4+10
17. 7+10
Q and A
18. 9+10
19. 10+6
20. 0+10
21. 10+10
22. 10+2
23. 10+3
24. 10+5
25. 6+10
26. 10+5
27. 6+10
A only
28. 10+9
29. 8+10
30. 4+10
31. 10+2
32. 2+10

33. 9+10
34. 8+10
35. 1+10
36. 7+10
37. 5+10
Q and A
38. 5+10
39. 5+10
40. 8+10
41. 1+10
42. 2+10
43. 10+3
44. 4+10
45. 10+9
46. 10+1
47. 2+10
A only
48. 10+4
49. 10+5
50. 10+1
51. 3+10
52. 6+10
53. 4+10
54. 10+1
55. 10+6
56. 8+10
Q and A
57. 9+10
58. 10+5
59. 2+10
60. 10+6
61. 10+8
62. 10+3
63. 2+10
64. 10+10
65. 2+10

66. 8+10
A only
67. 9+10
68. 2+10
69. 10+3
70. 4+10
71. 3+10
72. 1+10
73. 1+10
74. 10+8
75. 8+10
76. 10+9
Q and A
77. 10+1
78. 0+10
79. 10+10
80. 2+10
81. 10+5
82. 10+1
83. 7+10
84. 10+8
85. 10+6
86. 1+10
87. 2+10
A only
88. 10+4
89. 2+10
90. 8+10
91. 10+3
92. 2+10
Q and A
93. 7+10
A only
94. 10+5
95. 10+6
96. 7+10

97. 9+10
98. 10+6
99. 10+2
100.10+0

Plus 10's, Set 2

Num and A
1. 0+10
2. 2+10
3. 10+5
4. 6+10
5. 6+10
6. 9+10
7. 4+10
8. 10+4
9. 8+10
10. 8+10
A only
11. 10+7
12. 1+10
13. 4+10
14. 2+10
15. 10+10
16. 10+2
17. 10+6
18. 2+10
19. 10+5
20. 10+4
Num and A
21. 10+1
22. 10+9
23. 10+0
24. 10+3
25. 3+10
26. 6+10
27. 6+10
28. 10+1
A only
29. 7+10
30. 8+10
31. 8+10

32. 3+10
33. 10+7
34. 10+5
35. 4+10
36. 10+0
37. 10+8
38. 10+0
39. 10+8
40. 1+10
Num and A
41. 5+10
42. 10+10
43. 10+10
44. 10+1
45. 10+8
46. 10+4
47. 10+9
48. 10+1
49. 10+3
50. 6+10
A only
51. 10+8
52. 0+10
53. 0+10
54. 10+10
55. 10+4
56. 5+10
57. 1+10
58. 10+7
59. 10+7
60. 1+10
Num and A
61. 5+10
62. 5+10
63. 1+10

64. 10+1
65. 10+8
66. 10+6
67. 10+8
68. 4+10
69. 10+1
70. 9+10
A only
71. 10+6
72. 10+2
73. 10+4
74. 2+10
75. 4+10
76. 10+9
77. 1+10
78. 3+10
79. 10+2
80. 5+10
81. 3+10
82. 10+1
83. 10+3
84. 10+9
Num and A
85. 10+6
86. 10+2
87. 10+0
88. 10+4
A only
89. 6+10
90. 5+10
91. 8+10
92. 8+10
93. 10+8
94. 10+9
95. 10+10

96. 10+3
97. 10+2
Num and A
98. 10+10
99. 10+8
100. 3+10

Doubles, Set 1

Q and A
1. 3+3
2. 10+10
3. 9+9
4. 3+3
5. 8+8
6. 5+5
7. 5+5
8. 6+6
A only
9. 8+8
10. 6+6
11. 6+6
12. 10+10
13. 3+3
14. 4+4
15. 0+0
16. 2+2
17. 1+1
18. 3+3
Q and A
19. 0+0
20. 5+5
21. 5+5
22. 4+4
23. 9+9
24. 2+2
25. 1+1
26. 7+7
27. 8+8
A only
28. 6+6
29. 3+3
30. 9+9
31. 0+0
32. 6+6

33. 3+3
34. 2+2
35. 2+2
Q and A
36. 1+1
37. 7+7
38. 0+0
39. 10+10
40. 2+2
41. 9+9
42. 4+4
43. 9+9
44. 0+0
45. 8+8
46. 8+8
A only
47. 4+4
48. 3+3
49. 6+6
50. 2+2
51. 1+1
52. 10+10
53. 3+3
Q and A
54. 5+5
55. 9+9
56. 7+7
57. 0+0
58. 5+5
59. 4+4
60. 9+9
61. 3+3
62. 8+8
A only
63. 7+7
64. 5+5

65. 1+1
66. 0+0
67. 0+0
68. 4+4
69. 7+7
70. 7+7
71. 5+5
72. 4+4
Q and A
73. 6+6
74. 2+2
75. 9+9
76. 4+4
77. 6+6
78. 8+8
79. 5+5
80. 9+9
81. 3+3
82. 4+4
A only
83. 9+9
84. 4+4
85. 5+5
86. 9+9
87. 0+0
88. 2+2
89. 8+8
90. 6+6
91. 1+1
92. 1+1
Q and A
93. 9+9
94. 9+9
95. 4+4
A only
96. 0+0

97. 8+8
98. 3+3
99. 9+9
100. 7+7

Doubles, Set 2

Num and A
1. 3+3
2. 6+6
3. 8+8
4. 2+2
5. 2+2
6. 7+7
7. 6+6
8. 5+5
9. 8+8
10. 5+5
A only
11. 2+2
12. 2+2
13. 10+10
14. 2+2
15. 1+1
16. 2+2
Num and A
17. 5+5
18. 2+2
19. 10+10
20. 5+5
21. 7+7
22. 4+4
23. 2+2
24. 3+3
25. 9+9
26. 3+3
27. 1+1
28. 6+6
A only
29. 7+7
30. 6+6
31. 10+10
32. 0+0

33. 7+7
34. 4+4
35. 1+1
36. 3+3
37. 5+5
38. 5+5
39. 10+10
40. 10+10
41. 3+3
42. 9+9
Num and A
43. 8+8
44. 4+4
45. 10+10
46. 7+7
47. 6+6
48. 0+0
49. 0+0
50. 0+0
51. 6+6
52. 7+7
A only
53. 9+9
54. 10+10
55. 9+9
56. 1+1
57. 7+7
58. 6+6
59. 3+3
60. 6+6
61. 0+0
Num and A
62. 0+0
63. 1+1
64. 10+10
65. 5+5

66. 1+1
67. 4+4
68. 2+2
69. 8+8
70. 2+2
71. 10+10
A only
72. 6+6
73. 3+3
74. 6+6
75. 3+3
76. 7+7
77. 5+5
78. 2+2
79. 10+10
80. 5+5
81. 4+4
Num and A
82. 4+4
83. 6+6
84. 10+10
85. 6+6
86. 1+1
87. 0+0
88. 1+1
89. 5+5
A only
90. 8+8
91. 3+3
92. 3+3
93. 9+9
94. 2+2
95. 2+2
96. 8+8
97. 2+2
98. 8+8

99. 7+7
100. 7+7

One aparts

A only
1. 3+2
2. 6+5
3. 7+8
4. 1+2
5. 5+6
6. 7+8
7. 10+9
8. 3+2
9. 5+4
10. 9+8

Q and A
11. 8+7
12. 9+8
13. 9+10
14. 8+7
15. 7+6
16. 7+8
17. 3+2
18. 9+10

A only
19. 4+5
20. 7+8
21. 5+6
22. 5+4
23. 9+10
24. 9+8
25. 3+4
26. 4+5
27. 5+4

Q and A
28. 3+4
29. 8+9
30. 1+2
31. 4+5
32. 3+2

33. 3+2
34. 3+2
35. 5+6
36. 10+9
37. 9+8

A only
38. 7+8
39. 9+10
40. 9+8
41. 2+1
42. 7+8
43. 3+4
44. 10+9
45. 2+1

Q and A
46. 2+1
47. 2+1
48. 3+4
49. 6+7
50. 8+7
51. 7+6
52. 4+5
53. 8+7
54. 6+7

A only
55. 3+2
56. 10+9
57. 7+8
58. 9+10
59. 2+1
60. 2+3
61. 4+3
62. 3+2
63. 3+2
64. 7+8
65. 9+10

Q and A
66. 4+3
67. 1+2
68. 6+5
69. 4+5
70. 5+4
71. 4+3
72. 3+2
73. 9+10
74. 7+6

A only
75. 7+8
76. 5+4
77. 4+5
78. 9+10
79. 8+9
80. 7+6
81. 10+9
82. 3+4
83. 7+8
84. 5+6
85. 2+3

Q and A
86. 7+8
87. 5+4
88. 8+9
89. 10+9
90. 7+8
91. 6+7
92. 10+9
93. 8+9
94. 9+8
95. 10+9
96. 2+1
97. 6+5
98. 3+2

99. 10+9
A only
100. 6+7

Two Aparts

Num and A	33. 0+2	65. 5+7	97. 7+5
1. 8+10	34. 9+7	66. 3+5	98. 2+4
2. 3+5	35. 5+3	67. 4+6	99. 4+6
3. 3+1	36. 7+9	68. 6+4	100. 6+8
4. 9+7	Num and A	69. 2+0	
5. 4+2	37. 3+1	70. 2+0	
6. 1+3	38. 2+0	Num and A	
7. 3+1	39. 6+4	71. 4+2	
8. 2+4	40. 8+10	72. 3+5	
9. 4+2	41. 2+4	73. 10+8	
10. 3+1	42. 3+1	74. 7+5	
11. 2+0	43. 4+6	75. 7+5	
A only	A only	76. 10+8	
12. 5+3	44. 3+5	77. 10+8	
13. 8+10	45. 0+2	78. 9+7	
14. 2+0	46. 8+10	79. 4+2	
15. 8+6	47. 3+1	80. 1+3	
16. 5+3	48. 1+3	A only	
17. 4+2	49. 3+1	81. 8+10	
18. 2+0	50. 4+6	82. 6+4	
19. 2+4	51. 7+5	83. 2+0	
20. 9+7	52. 3+5	84. 10+8	
21. 1+3	53. 3+5	85. 4+6	
Num and A	Num and A	86. 3+5	
22. 2+4	54. 6+8	87. 3+5	
23. 5+7	55. 8+10	88. 2+4	
24. 7+9	56. 5+3	89. 5+7	
25. 4+6	57. 7+5	90. 3+5	
26. 2+0	58. 5+3	Num and A	
27. 3+1	59. 6+8	91. 4+6	
A only	60. 8+10	92. 7+5	
28. 3+1	61. 2+4	93. 10+8	
29. 1+3	62. 0+2	94. 3+1	
30. 3+5	A only	95. 8+6	
31. 4+6	63. 5+7	96. 6+8	
32. 6+4	64. 9+7	A only	

Plus 9's

A only
1. 9+0
2. 9+6
3. 9+9
4. 9+3
5. 9+9
6. 1+9
7. 9+8
8. 9+8
Q and A
9. 9+6
10. 7+9
11. 9+7
12. 9+7
13. 1+9
A only
14. 9+2
15. 9+7
16. 9+2
17. 0+9
18. 9+5
19. 9+9
20. 4+9
Q and A
21. 9+1
22. 4+9
23. 9+6
24. 9+9
25. 8+9
26. 5+9
27. 0+9
28. 6+9
29. 8+9
30. 9+4
31. 9+10
32. 9+4

33. 9+7
34. 1+9
35. 8+9
A only
36. 4+9
37. 9+0
38. 6+9
39. 6+9
40. 9+1
41. 4+9
42. 9+1
43. 6+9
44. 9+10
45. 3+9
46. 9+5
47. 9+6
48. 9+0
Q and A
49. 4+9
50. 1+9
51. 9+9
52. 1+9
53. 6+9
54. 10+9
55. 5+9
56. 0+9
57. 3+9
58. 5+9
59. 8+9
60. 9+4
A only
61. 4+9
62. 8+9
63. 9+0
64. 9+8
65. 9+5

66. 9+10
67. 4+9
68. 7+9
69. 8+9
70. 8+9
71. 9+2
Q and A
72. 1+9
73. 1+9
74. 0+9
75. 9+9
76. 9+9
77. 9+0
78. 7+9
79. 9+5
A only
80. 4+9
81. 9+6
82. 9+9
83. 2+9
84. 9+3
85. 9+10
86. 9+0
87. 6+9
88. 8+9
89. 9+4
90. 9+6
Q and A
91. 8+9
92. 5+9
93. 1+9
94. 9+8
95. 8+9
96. 8+9
97. 9+1
98. 9+4

99. 7+9
100. 9+7

The Remaining Six

Num and A
1. 8+3
2. 5+8
3. 4+7
4. 3+8
5. 7+4
6. 3+6
7. 8+3
8. 7+3
9. 4+7
10. 4+7
11. 4+8
A only
12. 6+3
13. 8+5
14. 5+8
15. 3+6
16. 8+3
17. 8+3
18. 4+7
19. 4+7
20. 5+8
21. 8+5
Num and A
22. 4+7
23. 3+7
24. 3+8
25. 3+7
26. 3+8
27. 3+6
28. 3+7
29. 7+3
30. 3+6
31. 8+5
32. 5+8
A only

33. 4+7
34. 5+8
35. 3+7
36. 7+3
37. 8+5
38. 4+8
39. 6+3
40. 7+3
Num and A
41. 4+7
42. 6+3
43. 8+5
44. 6+3
45. 5+8
46. 4+8
47. 3+8
48. 7+3
49. 5+8
50. 4+7
51. 8+4
52. 4+8
53. 3+8
A only
54. 8+3
55. 8+5
56. 5+8
57. 7+4
58. 5+8
59. 8+3
60. 4+7
61. 6+3
62. 4+7
63. 8+4
64. 4+8
65. 3+8
Num and A

66. 5+8
67. 8+5
68. 8+4
69. 7+4
70. 4+7
71. 8+5
72. 4+7
A only
73. 8+3
74. 6+3
75. 3+7
76. 8+3
77. 5+8
78. 3+7
79. 8+5
80. 6+3
81. 3+8
82. 3+8
83. 8+5
84. 8+5
85. 8+3
86. 7+4
87. 3+6
Num and A
88. 4+8
89. 6+3
90. 8+4
91. 8+4
92. 8+5
93. 7+4
94. 7+4
95. 5+8
A only
96. 6+3
97. 4+8
98. 4+8

99. 8+5
100. 8+3

All Addition Facts, Set 1

Q and A
1. 2+7
2. 2+6
3. 9+10
4. 6+9
5. 8+10
6. 3+3
7. 8+9
8. 7+10
9. 8+8
10. 5+7
11. 9+10
12. 0+0
13. 0+8
A only
14. 5+7
15. 4+9
16. 7+10
17. 1+10
18. 3+8
19. 6+10
20. 1+10
21. 9+9
22. 5+10
23. 2+2
Q and A
24. 8+9
25. 5+8
26. 4+10
27. 6+8
28. 0+7
29. 0+9
30. 3+8
A only
31. 8+10
32. 2+10

33. 1+10
34. 6+6
35. 2+3
36. 5+7
37. 4+5
38. 2+3
39. 3+4
40. 1+7
41. 3+5
42. 2+7
Q and A
43. 1+5
44. 8+9
45. 1+3
46. 8+8
47. 6+8
48. 10+10
49. 2+10
50. 1+1
51. 3+6
52. 2+7
53. 1+9
A only
54. 3+10
55. 1+9
56. 1+1
57. 8+9
58. 4+5
59. 4+8
60. 5+5
61. 2+9
Q and A
62. 9+10
63. 4+9
64. 5+7
65. 1+1

66. 2+6
67. 1+3
68. 6+10
69. 8+10
70. 2+10
71. 1+4
72. 3+5
A only
73. 4+9
74. 4+6
75. 0+2
76. 2+10
77. 2+9
78. 0+8
79. 1+1
80. 1+9
81. 6+6
82. 2+8
83. 7+8
84. 4+8
85. 1+9
86. 4+7
87. 0+8
Q and A
88. 3+3
89. 1+7
90. 2+2
91. 8+10
92. 6+10
93. 4+4
94. 3+7
95. 0+0
A only
96. 2+10
97. 4+5
98. 4+4

99. 2+6
100. 4+10

All Addition Facts, Set 2

A only
1. 8+7
2. 5+0
3. 6+7
4. 3+9
5. 2+1
Num and A
6. 0+7
7. 2+9
8. 0+9
9. 3+1
10. 10+2
11. 4+6
12. 5+7
13. 5+5
A only
14. 7+7
15. 10+7
16. 5+9
17. 10+5
18. 4+3
19. 8+2
20. 6+8
21. 8+3
22. 8+0
23. 8+1
24. 5+3
25. 1+6
26. 2+5
27. 5+6
28. 7+9
Num and A
29. 0+8
30. 4+1
31. 2+10
32. 9+3

33. 7+2
34. 10+1
35. 8+8
A only
36. 8+4
37. 7+8
38. 9+2
39. 10+10
40. 2+4
41. 3+5
42. 0+2
43. 3+10
44. 4+8
45. 8+5
46. 9+10
47. 3+6
Num and A
48. 8+9
49. 3+4
50. 6+1
51. 0+5
52. 0+1
53. 9+6
54. 5+8
55. 0+0
56. 9+8
57. 1+9
58. 1+8
59. 2+6
60. 3+8
A only
61. 6+4
62. 1+10
63. 6+0
64. 4+7
65. 6+2

66. 4+10
67. 10+3
68. 4+5
Num and A
69. 8+10
70. 9+1
71. 1+3
72. 1+1
73. 1+5
74. 4+2
75. 9+4
76. 1+7
77. 4+9
78. 10+6
79. 6+6
A only
80. 3+2
81. 10+9
82. 9+0
83. 7+6
84. 8+6
85. 0+6
86. 9+5
87. 4+4
88. 0+3
89. 2+3
Num and A
90. 5+1
91. 10+4
92. 2+7
93. 3+3
94. 7+4
95. 6+3
96. 6+5
97. 7+1
98. 4+0

99. 9+9
100. 3+7

All Addition Facts, Set 3

For "Sum-1st=2nd," when you see 2+7, say "9 minus 2 equals 7."

Sum-1st=2nd
1. 9+7
2. 8+6
3. 6+3
4. 6+1
5. 1+10
6. 0+2
7. 7+0
A only
8. 6+8
9. 7+10
10. 1+4
11. 8+7
12. 3+9
13. 3+1
14. 5+6
15. 8+0
Sum-1st=2nd
16. 6+2
17. 10+6
18. 9+4
19. 3+2
20. 10+10
21. 2+10
22. 7+5
23. 6+6
24. 2+0
A only
25. 7+6
26. 7+4
27. 10+8
28. 8+3
29. 5+1
30. 9+6
31. 4+10

32. 4+1
33. 4+8
34. 6+0
35. 7+9
36. 3+5
Sum-1st=2nd
37. 0+7
38. 9+5
39. 9+3
40. 2+5
41. 0+1
42. 0+3
43. 9+2
44. 0+5
45. 2+2
46. 0+9
A only
47. 6+9
48. 2+6
49. 10+2
50. 7+1
51. 1+9
52. 8+10
Sum-1st=2nd
53. 1+2
54. 3+8
55. 10+0
56. 9+8
57. 9+9
58. 6+5
59. 1+1
60. 3+0
61. 2+8
62. 7+2
63. 1+8

64. 4+6
A only
65. 5+4
66. 9+1
67. 10+5
68. 8+8
69. 2+9
70. 3+3
71. 3+10
72. 10+7
73. 9+0
74. 2+1
Sum-1st=2nd
75. 3+4
76. 6+10
77. 9+10
78. 4+9
79. 8+4
A only
80. 0+4
81. 1+6
82. 4+2
83. 1+5
84. 1+7
85. 8+2
86. 4+3
Sum-1st=2nd
87. 1+3
88. 2+3
89. 4+4
90. 8+9
91. 0+6
92. 4+5
93. 5+7
A only

94. 7+3
95. 4+7
96. 8+5
97. 5+5
98. 7+7
99. 5+9
100. 1+0

All Addition Facts, Set 4

A only
1. 2+4
2. 0+9
3. 2+7
4. 6+3
5. 8+8
6. 9+5
7. 5+10
8. 2+1
9. 9+7
10. 10+2
11. 3+8
12. 8+9
Sum-1st=2nd
13. 7+1
14. 2+10
15. 5+9
16. 0+3
17. 9+1
18. 3+0
19. 10+6
20. 9+2
21. 4+5
22. 7+4
A only
23. 8+10
24. 10+8
25. 4+7
26. 7+8
27. 9+3
28. 6+2
29. 6+0
30. 2+3
31. 5+4
32. 3+9
33. 1+2

34. 5+0
35. 4+8
36. 6+4
Sum-1st=2nd
37. 4+4
38. 9+0
39. 6+6
40. 9+10
41. 8+2
42. 1+7
43. 5+2
44. 2+5
45. 9+9
46. 0+0
47. 8+0
A only
48. 1+8
49. 7+2
50. 8+6
51. 0+4
52. 7+9
Sum-1st=2nd
53. 10+4
54. 6+1
55. 10+9
56. 4+9
57. 1+10
58. 6+7
59. 7+7
60. 7+10
61. 0+6
62. 1+6
63. 5+8
A only
64. 8+7
65. 7+6

66. 8+5
67. 8+1
68. 0+1
69. 4+1
70. 10+3
71. 0+8
72. 5+6
73. 5+5
Sum-1st=2nd
74. 2+2
75. 3+10
76. 6+10
77. 2+8
78. 9+8
79. 7+3
80. 1+1
81. 0+7
82. 2+0
83. 7+0
84. 1+5
85. 8+4
A only
86. 0+2
87. 1+0
88. 10+7
89. 5+7
90. 0+5
Sum-1st=2nd
91. 2+9
92. 3+4
93. 3+5
94. 7+5
95. 10+5
96. 1+3
A only
97. 4+0

98. 3+3
99. 10+10
100. 9+4

Subtraction Facts

All Subtraction Facts, Set 1

A only
1. 6-6
2. 5-5
3. 10-4
4. 9-6
5. 18-8

Q and A
6. 9-5
7. 17-7
8. 5-2
9. 6-4
10. 10-5
11. 5-1
12. 12-6
13. 16-7

A only
14. 6-2
15. 3-0
16. 10-7
17. 9-0
18. 9-3
19. 9-9
20. 14-7
21. 9-2
22. 4-3
23. 6-1
24. 10-10
25. 11-9
26. 19-9
27. 3-3
28. 20-10

Q and A
29. 11-10
30. 11-3

31. 7-3
32. 3-1
33. 8-3
34. 6-5
35. 13-9

A only
36. 18-10
37. 15-6
38. 11-6
39. 13-4
40. 7-2
41. 9-8
42. 14-5
43. 7-5
44. 11-7
45. 6-3
46. 15-9
47. 12-10

Q and A
48. 12-4
49. 8-4
50. 15-5
51. 14-9
52. 11-2
53. 9-7
54. 10-9
55. 14-10
56. 15-7
57. 2-0
58. 13-7
59. 4-4
60. 5-4

A only
61. 10-1

62. 14-4
63. 17-10
64. 12-8
65. 7-6
66. 16-9
67. 7-0
68. 11-5

Q and A
69. 13-6
70. 8-0
71. 10-2
72. 2-1
73. 19-10
74. 16-8
75. 10-8
76. 7-4
77. 6-0
78. 8-7
79. 15-10

A only
80. 0-0
81. 5-0
82. 13-10
83. 17-8
84. 14-6
85. 4-2
86. 12-2
87. 8-6
88. 15-8
89. 1-0

Q and A
90. 5-3
91. 12-9
92. 11-1

93. 13-5
94. 11-4
95. 9-4
96. 12-7
97. 7-7
98. 2-2
99. 1-1
100. 16-10

All Subtraction Facts, Set 2

Q and A
1. 11-4
2. 15-6
3. 16-9
4. 7-6
5. 18-9
6. 11-8
7. 9-8
8. 6-2
9. 7-1
10. 5-2
A only
11. 4-1
12. 11-2
13. 9-0
14. 7-3
15. 10-6
16. 14-10
17. 3-0
18. 2-0
19. 11-5
20. 6-3
21. 7-5
Q and A
22. 12-3
23. 10-4
24. 3-2
25. 10-2
26. 11-7
27. 3-1
28. 12-7
29. 2-2
A only
30. 3-3
31. 12-5
32. 10-10

33. 11-3
34. 10-7
35. 9-5
36. 5-0
37. 17-7
38. 10-9
39. 11-10
40. 16-8
Q and A
41. 18-10
42. 6-5
43. 12-2
44. 5-1
45. 7-4
46. 5-4
47. 17-8
48. 13-3
49. 8-4
50. 6-0
51. 19-10
52. 10-5
A only
53. 10-3
54. 15-7
55. 7-7
56. 14-9
57. 13-4
58. 7-0
59. 9-9
60. 4-3
61. 8-1
62. 13-10
63. 11-6
64. 4-2
65. 11-1
Q and A

66. 15-8
67. 13-7
68. 14-7
69. 12-8
70. 6-1
71. 9-7
72. 6-4
73. 8-2
74. 14-5
75. 10-1
76. 10-0
77. 8-0
78. 5-3
79. 9-3
80. 9-1
A only
81. 1-1
82. 10-8
83. 4-4
84. 18-8
85. 8-7
86. 9-2
87. 16-7
Q and A
88. 1-0
89. 12-9
90. 14-4
91. 12-10
92. 4-0
A only
93. 14-6
94. 15-9
95. 13-9
96. 5-5
97. 6-6
98. 9-4

99. 0-0
100. 13-6

All Subtraction Facts, Set 3

Num and A
1. 15-5
2. 8-8
3. 19-9
4. 16-7
5. 12-6
A only
6. 14-7
7. 12-2
8. 5-0
9. 8-5
10. 2-1
11. 13-5
12. 2-2
13. 7-1
Num and A
14. 7-5
15. 9-4
16. 13-6
17. 9-7
18. 12-5
19. 11-2
20. 12-9
21. 18-9
22. 5-2
23. 11-8
24. 20-10
25. 10-6
26. 11-7
27. 15-9
28. 8-2
A only
29. 14-10
30. 3-0
31. 10-10
32. 6-3

33. 7-0
34. 8-1
35. 13-9
Num and A
36. 3-1
37. 3-3
38. 16-9
39. 16-6
40. 10-7
41. 4-4
42. 12-7
43. 9-6
44. 2-0
45. 18-10
46. 0-0
47. 6-6
A only
48. 9-8
49. 10-0
50. 10-3
51. 8-0
52. 9-0
53. 16-10
54. 11-1
55. 16-8
56. 1-1
57. 10-4
58. 12-4
59. 9-9
60. 6-1
Num and A
61. 5-4
62. 10-9
63. 12-3
64. 11-5
65. 5-3

66. 18-8
67. 3-2
68. 13-8
A only
69. 1-0
70. 11-9
71. 6-4
72. 19-10
73. 7-2
74. 12-10
75. 11-4
76. 8-3
77. 11-10
78. 15-6
79. 17-10
Num and A
80. 14-6
81. 10-5
82. 7-3
83. 4-2
84. 8-4
85. 10-2
86. 14-9
87. 6-2
88. 8-6
89. 12-8
A only
90. 15-8
91. 17-8
92. 13-4
93. 17-7
94. 6-0
95. 5-5
96. 9-1
97. 14-4
98. 13-10

99. 14-5
100. 10-8

All Subtraction Facts, Set 4

A only
1. 9-2
2. 12-8
3. 6-5
4. 13-8
5. 5-5
6. 12-6
7. 9-8
8. 11-7

Q and A
9. 11-6
10. 17-10
11. 10-10
12. 14-8
13. 7-6
14. 13-9
15. 0-0
16. 15-8
17. 10-4
18. 12-3
19. 6-4
20. 5-1

A only
21. 10-0
22. 1-1
23. 15-9
24. 6-6
25. 17-7
26. 16-7
27. 10-3
28. 4-1
29. 2-0
30. 8-8
31. 9-3
32. 5-2
33. 8-7

Q and A
34. 5-4
35. 13-4
36. 13-3
37. 7-7
38. 18-9
39. 14-5
40. 3-3
41. 4-0
42. 9-7
43. 6-1
44. 12-2
45. 14-9
46. 10-8
47. 8-4
48. 10-6

A only
49. 7-4
50. 16-10
51. 3-2
52. 7-2
53. 4-2
54. 6-3
55. 9-6
56. 11-3
57. 4-4
58. 13-7
59. 12-7

Q and A
60. 11-5
61. 6-2
62. 11-2
63. 3-0
64. 16-6
65. 4-3
66. 14-6

67. 6-0

A only
68. 12-9
69. 14-10
70. 8-5
71. 11-8
72. 19-10
73. 11-10
74. 1-0

Q and A
75. 9-1
76. 15-5
77. 17-9
78. 7-1
79. 18-8

A only
80. 16-8
81. 14-4
82. 13-10
83. 15-10
84. 2-2
85. 10-5
86. 17-8
87. 9-0
88. 12-4
89. 7-3
90. 7-0

Q and A
91. 12-5
92. 10-7
93. 9-5
94. 5-3
95. 10-9
96. 8-3
97. 15-6
98. 9-9

99. 14-7
100. 2-1

All Subtraction Facts, Set 5

A only
1. 3-0
2. 16-8
3. 17-7
4. 10-0
5. 9-9
6. 13-5
7. 10-3
8. 7-5
9. 8-7
10. 7-1
11. 5-4
Num and A
12. 9-0
13. 11-1
14. 5-1
15. 6-2
16. 0-0
17. 9-1
18. 4-1
19. 13-3
20. 11-5
21. 11-7
A only
22. 12-5
23. 3-2
24. 7-0
25. 12-8
26. 11-2
27. 14-4
28. 8-0
29. 8-2
30. 8-6
31. 13-8
32. 15-6
Q and A

33. 17-8
34. 19-9
35. 12-9
36. 10-6
37. 15-9
38. 8-1
39. 13-6
40. 9-3
A only
41. 10-10
42. 18-8
43. 2-1
44. 20-10
45. 10-1
46. 15-10
47. 1-1
48. 18-9
49. 12-4
50. 3-3
51. 10-4
52. 14-10
53. 13-10
Q and A
54. 10-9
55. 7-2
56. 9-4
57. 12-10
58. 6-3
59. 5-5
60. 11-6
61. 13-9
62. 1-0
63. 2-0
64. 16-9
65. 16-6
A only

66. 5-2
67. 6-1
68. 18-10
69. 14-8
70. 13-4
71. 11-3
72. 11-9
Q and A
73. 5-0
74. 7-7
75. 17-9
76. 17-10
77. 4-3
78. 8-8
79. 9-8
80. 13-7
81. 10-2
82. 9-7
83. 11-8
84. 8-5
85. 8-3
86. 19-10
87. 10-5
A only
88. 12-6
89. 12-3
90. 4-0
91. 7-4
92. 10-7
93. 7-3
94. 6-5
95. 3-1
Q and A
96. 10-8
97. 14-9
98. 12-7

99. 6-4
100. 6-6

Multiplication Facts

Times 0's, 1's, and 2's

Num and A
1. 8x0
2. 7x2
3. 2x0
4. 6x0
5. 0x5
6. 0x9
7. 2x6
8. 2x4
9. 1x6
10. 2x9
A only
11. 0x3
12. 7x1
13. 2x4
14. 0x1
15. 2x7
16. 8x0
17. 7x0
18. 4x1
Num and A
19. 7x1
20. 9x0
21. 0x5
22. 7x2
23. 2x4
24. 2x4
25. 1x3
26. 2x2
27. 7x2
A only
28. 9x0
29. 1x4
30. 10x1

31. 4x0
32. 6x1
33. 2x2
34. 8x1
35. 5x1
36. 2x0
37. 1x2
Num and A
38. 1x10
39. 0x9
40. 10x0
41. 1x5
42. 0x6
43. 2x2
44. 1x0
45. 2x7
A only
46. 9x1
47. 6x1
48. 8x0
49. 1x3
50. 2x1
51. 3x2
52. 10x0
53. 9x1
54. 0x2
Num and A
55. 1x7
56. 0x6
57. 8x2
58. 0x4
59. 7x0
60. 2x0
61. 1x4

62. 1x1
63. 2x2
64. 2x2
65. 0x10
A only
66. 5x0
67. 0x9
68. 1x0
69. 0x8
70. 1x1
71. 0x8
72. 1x2
73. 9x1
74. 3x2
Num and A
75. 7x0
76. 6x2
77. 2x9
78. 10x0
79. 0x6
80. 2x7
81. 1x6
82. 4x1
83. 2x1
84. 1x3
85. 5x1
A only
86. 1x8
87. 3x1
88. 1x8
89. 7x0
90. 4x0
91. 1x5
92. 2x9

93. 0x2
94. 1x10
95. 0x5
96. 0x5
97. 2x9
98. 1x4
99. 9x0
Num and A
100. 8x0

Times 10's

Q and A
1. 3x10
2. 10x9
3. 10x7
4. 10x6
5. 10x3
6. 10x7
7. 9x10
8. 8x10
9. 10x5
10. 10x3
11. 5x10
A only
12. 10x3
13. 4x10
14. 5x10
15. 6x10
16. 4x10
17. 10x9
18. 10x9
19. 10x10
20. 2x10
21. 10x7
Q and A
22. 10x0
23. 10x0
24. 6x10
25. 8x10
26. 6x10
27. 0x10
A only
28. 5x10
29. 10x4
30. 0x10
31. 10x3
32. 2x10

33. 5x10
34. 2x10
35. 4x10
36. 10x6
Q and A
37. 9x10
38. 8x10
39. 2x10
40. 3x10
41. 10x3
42. 10x7
43. 6x10
A only
44. 5x10
45. 10x3
46. 8x10
47. 5x10
48. 10x3
49. 7x10
50. 10x5
51. 3x10
52. 10x2
53. 10x0
Q and A
54. 6x10
55. 10x4
56. 10x5
57. 10x5
58. 2x10
59. 9x10
60. 1x10
61. 10x5
62. 5x10
A only
63. 10x9
64. 10x10

65. 8x10
66. 10x0
67. 5x10
68. 8x10
69. 10x7
70. 10x0
Q and A
71. 3x10
72. 10x0
73. 0x10
74. 7x10
75. 9x10
76. 3x10
77. 10x1
78. 2x10
79. 10x2
80. 10x2
A only
81. 8x10
82. 10x7
83. 3x10
84. 10x1
85. 5x10
86. 10x3
87. 10x2
88. 8x10
89. 10x10
90. 0x10
Q and A
91. 10x0
92. 10x2
93. 10x7
94. 8x10
95. 6x10
96. 10x5
A only

97. 10x6
98. 10x4
99. 8x10
100. 10x2

Times 3's

A only
1. 2x3
2. 0x3
3. 8x3
4. 3x10
5. 7x3
6. 1x3
7. 4x3
8. 3x3
Num and A
9. 3x8
10. 6x3
11. 3x1
12. 1x3
13. 3x10
A only
14. 3x0
15. 4x3
16. 6x3
17. 8x3
18. 6x3
19. 1x3
20. 3x2
Num and A
21. 3x7
22. 3x3
23. 7x3
24. 1x3
25. 7x3
26. 7x3
27. 6x3
28. 3x5
29. 0x3
30. 8x3
31. 3x8
32. 10x3
33. 7x3
34. 3x4
35. 9x3
A only
36. 3x2
37. 5x3
38. 3x8
39. 9x3
40. 3x4
41. 2x3
42. 3x8
43. 8x3
44. 10x3
45. 3x6
46. 6x3
47. 6x3
48. 0x3
Num and A
49. 1x3
50. 0x3
51. 3x2
52. 1x3
53. 3x8
54. 3x7
55. 10x3
56. 5x3
57. 3x5
58. 10x3
59. 3x2
60. 4x3
A only
61. 2x3
62. 3x1
63. 0x3
64. 8x3
65. 3x2
66. 9x3
67. 3x6
68. 3x6
69. 8x3
70. 3x10
71. 3x4
Num and A
72. 3x7
73. 3x7
74. 2x3
75. 9x3
76. 3x3
77. 3x1
78. 9x3
79. 6x3
A only
80. 3x10
81. 1x3
82. 4x3
83. 3x4
84. 3x8
85. 9x3
86. 3x0
87. 0x3
88. 3x8
89. 3x8
90. 2x3
Num and A
91. 4x3
92. 4x3
93. 3x2
94. 3x4
95. 1x3
96. 3x3
97. 5x3
98. 8x3
99. 1x3
100. 3x0

Times 4's

A only
1. 5x4
2. 10x4
3. 5x4
4. 4x7
5. 4x10
6. 2x4
7. 3x4
8. 4x10
9. 8x4
10. 4x9
11. 3x4
Q and A
12. 7x4
13. 4x10
14. 4x0
15. 4x0
16. 5x4
17. 2x4
18. 4x8
19. 4x2
20. 4x9
21. 8x4
A only
22. 4x5
23. 5x4
24. 4x3
25. 4x6
26. 4x10
27. 10x4
28. 4x1
29. 4x6
30. 4x5
31. 0x4
32. 4x2
Q and A

33. 4x7
34. 4x9
35. 10x4
36. 7x4
37. 0x4
38. 4x0
39. 4x0
40. 4x5
A only
41. 4x2
42. 6x4
43. 0x4
44. 4x7
45. 4x8
46. 3x4
47. 4x2
48. 1x4
49. 4x2
50. 6x4
51. 4x9
52. 1x4
53. 4x5
Q and A
54. 6x4
55. 0x4
56. 4x6
57. 4x0
58. 4x3
59. 1x4
60. 4x1
61. 7x4
62. 4x9
63. 10x4
64. 4x8
65. 4x0
A only

66. 2x4
67. 0x4
68. 1x4
69. 4x4
70. 4x10
71. 4x8
72. 3x4
Q and A
73. 4x4
74. 2x4
75. 4x3
76. 3x4
77. 1x4
78. 2x4
79. 4x3
80. 4x4
81. 7x4
82. 8x4
83. 9x4
84. 4x5
85. 7x4
86. 8x4
87. 5x4
A only
88. 4x4
89. 0x4
90. 4x1
91. 4x9
92. 4x9
93. 9x4
94. 9x4
95. 4x1
Q and A
96. 4x3
97. 0x4
98. 10x4

99. 0x4
100. 7x4

Times 5's

Num and A
1. 5x9
2. 5x9
3. 5x7
4. 8x5
5. 8x5
6. 5x8
7. 2x5
8. 5x0
9. 10x5
10. 8x5
11. 5x1
12. 5x9
13. 7x5
A only
14. 5x7
15. 5x10
16. 4x5
17. 7x5
18. 5x10
19. 5x6
20. 5x7
21. 6x5
22. 5x7
23. 6x5
Num and A
24. 5x0
25. 5x3
26. 5x6
27. 8x5
28. 5x4
29. 0x5
30. 5x5
A only
31. 0x5
32. 5x2

33. 5x7
34. 9x5
35. 5x7
36. 7x5
37. 3x5
38. 5x5
39. 5x10
40. 7x5
41. 2x5
42. 5x6
Num and A
43. 4x5
44. 7x5
45. 5x6
46. 5x8
47. 5x0
48. 5x6
49. 2x5
50. 5x8
51. 3x5
52. 3x5
53. 8x5
A only
54. 5x2
55. 5x3
56. 4x5
57. 7x5
58. 5x3
59. 5x6
60. 2x5
61. 10x5
Num and A
62. 7x5
63. 5x3
64. 1x5
65. 0x5

66. 5x8
67. 9x5
68. 5x8
69. 5x5
70. 5x8
71. 5x8
72. 5x7
A only
73. 5x10
74. 5x4
75. 3x5
76. 7x5
77. 6x5
78. 5x7
79. 5x6
80. 5x4
81. 5x3
82. 5x0
83. 5x6
84. 8x5
85. 7x5
86. 5x1
87. 4x5
Num and A
88. 5x5
89. 3x5
90. 5x0
91. 6x5
92. 0x5
93. 4x5
94. 7x5
95. 5x10
A only
96. 5x6
97. 10x5
98. 4x5

99. 5x2
100. 4x5

Times 6's

A only
1. 6x6
2. 6x10
3. 6x10
4. 6x6
5. 9x6

Q and A
6. 3x6
7. 6x9
8. 6x1
9. 0x6
10. 6x10
11. 6x7
12. 8x6
13. 3x6

A only
14. 6x9
15. 1x6
16. 6x4
17. 4x6
18. 9x6
19. 6x0
20. 4x6
21. 2x6
22. 6x9
23. 6x6
24. 6x2
25. 6x3
26. 6x4
27. 9x6
28. 6x0

Q and A
29. 6x3
30. 7x6
31. 6x4
32. 10x6

33. 6x10
34. 0x6
35. 3x6

A only
36. 6x10
37. 2x6
38. 6x2
39. 6x10
40. 10x6
41. 2x6
42. 6x2
43. 3x6
44. 6x8
45. 6x6
46. 6x3
47. 5x6

Q and A
48. 2x6
49. 6x6
50. 6x2
51. 2x6
52. 6x1
53. 6x4
54. 6x1
55. 0x6
56. 7x6
57. 6x0
58. 4x6
59. 6x5
60. 4x6

A only
61. 2x6
62. 5x6
63. 6x4
64. 6x4
65. 5x6

66. 8x6
67. 10x6
68. 6x0

Q and A
69. 10x6
70. 0x6
71. 1x6
72. 6x9
73. 4x6
74. 5x6
75. 7x6
76. 6x8
77. 7x6
78. 6x6
79. 6x9

A only
80. 7x6
81. 2x6
82. 6x4
83. 7x6
84. 7x6
85. 6x6
86. 4x6
87. 10x6
88. 6x9
89. 1x6

Q and A
90. 6x8
91. 3x6
92. 3x6
93. 6x7
94. 6x3
95. 6x1
96. 1x6
97. 2x6
98. 4x6

99. 6x7
100. 6x9

Times 7's

A only
1. 9x7
2. 7x5
3. 7x7
4. 8x7
5. 7x0
6. 7x2
7. 7x6
8. 10x7
9. 4x7
10. 1x7
Num and A
11. 0x7
12. 4x7
13. 7x5
14. 3x7
15. 7x9
16. 7x8
17. 7x7
18. 5x7
19. 7x6
20. 7x6
21. 3x7
A only
22. 4x7
23. 9x7
24. 7x4
25. 7x9
26. 7x8
27. 7x5
28. 7x4
29. 7x7
Num and A
30. 1x7
31. 5x7
32. 10x7
33. 7x3
34. 0x7
35. 6x7
36. 7x1
37. 7x0
38. 6x7
39. 7x1
40. 4x7
A only
41. 7x2
42. 7x0
43. 6x7
44. 3x7
45. 7x2
46. 7x0
47. 7x10
48. 7x8
49. 0x7
50. 7x9
51. 6x7
52. 7x8
Num and A
53. 3x7
54. 7x6
55. 7x6
56. 7x9
57. 6x7
58. 6x7
59. 7x4
60. 6x7
61. 7x6
62. 7x5
63. 7x6
64. 2x7
65. 2x7
A only
66. 10x7
67. 8x7
68. 7x0
69. 7x0
70. 7x7
71. 2x7
72. 8x7
73. 7x0
74. 4x7
75. 6x7
76. 7x6
77. 8x7
78. 0x7
79. 10x7
80. 7x1
Num and A
81. 10x7
82. 1x7
83. 2x7
84. 7x3
85. 6x7
86. 7x5
87. 10x7
A only
88. 7x4
89. 7x7
90. 7x8
91. 3x7
92. 7x1
Num and A
93. 10x7
94. 7x3
95. 7x2
96. 7x7
97. 7x3
98. 7x4
99. 7x3
100. 7x6

Times 8's

Q and A
1. 0x8
2. 8x9
3. 8x3
4. 10x8
5. 8x4
6. 8x2
7. 8x10
8. 4x8
9. 5x8
10. 8x7
11. 0x8

A only
12. 1x8
13. 8x8
14. 8x3
15. 8x0
16. 7x8
17. 7x8
18. 8x8
19. 8x0
20. 1x8
21. 5x8
22. 8x8
23. 0x8

Q and A
24. 5x8
25. 8x5
26. 6x8
27. 8x9
28. 0x8
29. 8x1
30. 8x3
31. 2x8
32. 8x8
33. 7x8

34. 8x6

A only
35. 8x8
36. 8x7
37. 8x10
38. 2x8
39. 3x8
40. 8x5
41. 7x8
42. 8x5
43. 8x6
44. 8x7

Q and A
45. 8x7
46. 8x4
47. 8x8
48. 4x8
49. 8x4
50. 8x1
51. 9x8

A only
52. 6x8
53. 10x8
54. 9x8
55. 8x6
56. 8x5
57. 4x8
58. 8x6
59. 8x1
60. 8x9
61. 0x8
62. 8x9
63. 8x4
64. 8x10
65. 8x0
66. 3x8

Q and A
67. 8x8
68. 8x8
69. 5x8
70. 8x5
71. 6x8
72. 1x8
73. 3x8
74. 8x10
75. 8x2
76. 3x8
77. 7x8
78. 8x8
79. 8x9

A only
80. 2x8
81. 8x5
82. 8x5
83. 5x8
84. 8x2

Q and A
85. 2x8
86. 8x10
87. 6x8
88. 4x8
89. 8x3
90. 8x4
91. 1x8
92. 8x2

A only
93. 3x8
94. 7x8
95. 6x8
96. 8x9
97. 6x8
98. 8x5

99. 8x1
100. 7x8

Times 9's

A only
1. 9x7
2. 8x9
3. 9x2
4. 9x4
5. 9x7
6. 9x9
7. 2x9
8. 3x9
Num and A
9. 0x9
10. 9x10
11. 9x0
12. 9x8
13. 5x9
14. 4x9
15. 4x9
16. 10x9
17. 9x0
18. 9x9
19. 4x9
A only
20. 9x3
21. 9x8
22. 9x1
23. 9x1
24. 9x10
25. 9x0
26. 9x1
27. 9x3
28. 9x4
29. 2x9
30. 9x1
31. 9x8
Num and A
32. 3x9

33. 9x8
34. 2x9
35. 9x8
36. 9x4
37. 2x9
38. 1x9
39. 9x8
40. 5x9
41. 8x9
42. 10x9
43. 9x5
44. 9x0
A only
45. 9x7
46. 8x9
47. 8x9
48. 9x7
49. 5x9
50. 2x9
51. 9x5
52. 9x10
53. 9x2
54. 1x9
55. 9x2
56. 9x2
57. 9x4
58. 10x9
59. 2x9
Num and A
60. 9x8
61. 4x9
62. 9x0
63. 1x9
64. 9x8
65. 9x9
66. 0x9

67. 5x9
A only
68. 6x9
69. 9x6
70. 7x9
71. 9x1
72. 9x0
73. 9x1
74. 9x6
75. 8x9
76. 0x9
77. 2x9
Num and A
78. 9x5
79. 9x10
80. 9x8
81. 10x9
82. 7x9
83. 9x9
84. 9x0
85. 9x9
86. 5x9
87. 9x8
88. 10x9
A only
89. 6x9
90. 10x9
91. 2x9
92. 8x9
93. 9x1
94. 9x1
95. 9x7
Num and A
96. 9x1
97. 9x0
98. 9x3

99. 7x9
100. 9x8

All Multiplication Facts, Set 1

A only
1. 10x1
2. 6x3
3. 2x10
4. 9x1
5. 9x4
6. 5x4
7. 8x9
8. 7x5
9. 0x0
10. 8x1
Q and A
11. 4x2
12. 7x7
13. 2x5
14. 4x10
15. 2x7
16. 1x1
17. 8x6
18. 7x2
A only
19. 3x2
20. 5x1
21. 4x7
22. 5x3
23. 4x4
24. 8x10
25. 8x5
26. 8x8
27. 2x0
Q and A
28. 2x4
29. 9x7
30. 10x3
31. 0x5
32. 3x5

33. 10x5
34. 6x8
35. 1x2
36. 1x6
37. 10x9
A only
38. 5x7
39. 0x4
40. 1x3
41. 2x6
42. 9x8
43. 5x8
44. 7x0
45. 0x8
Q and A
46. 8x2
47. 6x5
48. 7x10
49. 7x1
50. 2x2
51. 0x7
52. 9x9
53. 3x9
54. 6x2
A only
55. 6x0
56. 4x0
57. 10x2
58. 4x9
59. 3x10
60. 2x9
61. 10x10
62. 3x4
63. 9x2
64. 0x9
65. 1x4

Q and A
66. 10x7
67. 6x10
68. 5x0
69. 10x4
70. 2x1
71. 1x10
72. 6x9
73. 7x3
74. 10x0
A only
75. 0x3
76. 6x6
77. 5x10
78. 4x6
79. 4x5
80. 9x0
81. 4x8
82. 4x3
83. 8x7
84. 3x1
85. 7x8
Q and A
86. 2x3
87. 8x4
88. 1x7
89. 5x5
90. 7x4
91. 5x6
92. 6x4
93. 9x5
94. 7x6
95. 3x0
96. 1x9
97. 8x3
98. 0x6

99. 9x3
A only
100. 1x8

All Multiplication Facts, Set 2

A only
1. 7x5
2. 6x7
3. 7x7
4. 0x0
5. 5x10
6. 7x4
7. 1x2
8. 3x8
9. 0x3
10. 3x4
11. 9x2

Num and A
12. 4x6
13. 7x2
14. 9x10
15. 2x5
16. 3x0
17. 3x9
18. 9x8
19. 5x9
20. 3x7
21. 6x6

A only
22. 8x3
23. 6x10
24. 1x1
25. 4x3
26. 10x6
27. 1x6

Num and A
28. 1x4
29. 2x8
30. 9x5
31. 7x8
32. 2x10

33. 2x3
34. 0x9
35. 2x6
36. 8x0

A only
37. 10x9
38. 7x10
39. 4x1
40. 10x4
41. 4x9
42. 10x8
43. 6x0

Num and A
44. 5x2
45. 0x1
46. 1x7
47. 9x1
48. 6x2
49. 9x4
50. 9x9
51. 8x7
52. 1x9
53. 1x10

A only
54. 7x6
55. 0x5
56. 7x3
57. 2x2
58. 2x1
59. 10x1
60. 8x5
61. 10x0
62. 5x7

Num and A
63. 4x7
64. 1x3

65. 5x1
66. 0x4
67. 0x6
68. 9x6
69. 7x1
70. 0x8

A only
71. 5x8
72. 3x3
73. 10x3
74. 7x9
75. 4x0
76. 1x5
77. 3x2
78. 1x8
79. 3x5
80. 7x0

Num and A
81. 5x3
82. 6x1
83. 6x3
84. 9x3
85. 6x9
86. 4x2
87. 9x7
88. 10x2
89. 0x7
90. 6x5

A only
91. 8x10
92. 2x0
93. 6x8
94. 4x10
95. 8x2
96. 5x6

Num and A

97. 4x8
98. 3x10
99. 9x0
100. 0x10

All Multiplication Facts, Set 3

Q and A
1. 7x4
2. 6x6
3. 7x6
4. 10x6
5. 3x5
6. 2x10
7. 1x4
8. 3x8
A only
9. 8x9
10. 3x2
11. 10x9
12. 2x9
13. 0x10
Q and A
14. 10x2
15. 6x10
16. 10x1
17. 10x10
18. 8x8
19. 2x6
20. 9x5
A only
21. 10x3
22. 3x3
23. 3x0
24. 6x7
25. 10x7
26. 8x2
27. 0x7
28. 3x6
29. 5x6
30. 6x8
31. 4x10
32. 1x0

33. 4x0
34. 1x7
35. 1x8
Q and A
36. 8x4
37. 4x4
38. 0x0
39. 1x9
40. 0x3
41. 3x7
42. 7x3
43. 3x1
44. 9x10
45. 9x2
46. 2x3
47. 6x5
48. 1x2
A only
49. 10x4
50. 9x7
51. 4x5
52. 1x10
53. 7x7
54. 5x10
55. 3x10
56. 3x4
57. 5x5
58. 3x9
59. 4x1
60. 8x1
Q and A
61. 7x8
62. 10x0
63. 0x8
64. 2x4
65. 7x5

66. 0x4
67. 5x7
68. 1x5
69. 1x1
70. 5x3
71. 10x5
A only
72. 5x9
73. 0x6
74. 8x5
75. 0x2
76. 8x6
77. 2x1
78. 1x3
79. 2x2
Q and A
80. 9x4
81. 9x6
82. 7x1
83. 6x4
84. 8x10
85. 5x1
86. 9x9
87. 2x8
88. 4x7
89. 4x6
90. 5x8
A only
91. 4x2
92. 6x9
93. 9x3
94. 2x5
95. 1x6
96. 5x2
97. 2x7
98. 2x0

99. 6x1
100. 0x9

All Multiplication Facts, Set 4

Num and A
1. 1x6
2. 2x3
3. 8x0
4. 0x2
5. 1x10
6. 7x6
7. 7x4
8. 7x10
9. 4x6
10. 0x5
11. 6x10
A only
12. 5x7
13. 3x7
14. 6x4
15. 7x5
16. 5x3
17. 3x9
18. 1x1
19. 3x10
20. 0x8
21. 8x9
Num and A
22. 0x1
23. 4x7
24. 4x2
25. 7x9
26. 0x10
27. 10x2
28. 4x4
29. 5x5
30. 8x7
31. 9x6
32. 8x5
A only

33. 8x8
34. 10x3
35. 9x9
36. 2x7
37. 6x6
38. 0x4
39. 1x8
40. 2x6
Num and A
41. 2x8
42. 4x0
43. 7x0
44. 10x6
45. 0x3
46. 2x4
47. 7x7
48. 5x8
49. 10x8
50. 0x7
51. 3x2
52. 3x0
53. 8x4
A only
54. 7x3
55. 6x2
56. 10x4
57. 2x10
58. 9x1
59. 4x8
60. 6x1
61. 10x7
62. 2x5
63. 9x4
64. 10x1
65. 10x0
Num and A

66. 1x0
67. 0x9
68. 5x2
69. 1x9
70. 6x7
71. 10x10
72. 6x5
A only
73. 2x9
74. 4x9
75. 8x10
76. 9x8
77. 9x10
78. 7x2
79. 2x0
80. 1x2
81. 6x3
82. 9x7
83. 2x2
84. 4x1
85. 5x10
86. 5x1
87. 5x6
Num and A
88. 3x3
89. 4x3
90. 7x8
91. 0x0
92. 7x1
93. 3x5
94. 4x10
95. 5x9
A only
96. 9x0
97. 4x5
98. 3x6

99. 1x5
100. 9x2

All Multiplication Facts, Set 5

For "P/1st=2nd," when you see 3x4, say "12 divided by 3 equals 4."

P/1st=2nd
1. 7x2
2. 4x9
3. 8x8
4. 9x5
5. 2x3
6. 3x10
7. 8x4
8. 9x7
9. 6x5
10. 6x1
11. 1x3
12. 1x7
13. 3x0
A only
14. 5x2
15. 10x6
16. 8x3
17. 4x0
18. 7x6
19. 4x2
20. 6x0
21. 1x5
22. 7x10
23. 3x0
P/1st=2nd
24. 10x3
25. 9x10
26. 6x10
27. 2x6
28. 6x3
29. 8x10
30. 6x6
A only
31. 8x2

32. 3x9
33. 10x0
34. 4x3
35. 7x8
36. 5x0
37. 7x3
38. 9x2
39. 10x10
40. 8x9
41. 1x2
42. 3x8
P/1st=2nd
43. 10x8
44. 6x4
45. 9x3
46. 9x9
47. 5x8
48. 9x8
49. 10x9
50. 10x4
51. 1x4
52. 2x1
53. 9x6
A only
54. 10x7
55. 7x5
56. 1x1
57. 2x0
58. 6x9
59. 3x5
60. 10x1
61. 4x5
P/1st=2nd
62. 10x2
63. 5x10

64. 4x10
65. 1x5
66. 2x5
67. 5x1
68. 6x2
69. 3x9
70. 5x9
71. 6x7
72. 8x5
A only
73. 2x9
74. 1x8
75. 7x0
76. 2x4
77. 9x0
78. 9x1
79. 3x2
80. 7x1
81. 6x8
82. 3x4
83. 10x0
84. 8x1
85. 3x1
86. 5x3
87. 8x0
P/1st=2nd
88. 9x4
89. 4x8
90. 2x2
91. 7x4
92. 8x8
93. 5x4
94. 4x6
95. 3x7
A only

96. 6x7
97. 9x5
98. 3x3
99. 2x10
100. 2x8

All Multiplication Facts, Set 6

A only
1. 7x7
2. 8x5
3. 6x5
4. 4x0
5. 4x7
P/1st=2nd
6. 4x3
7. 8x1
8. 3x4
9. 5x9
10. 7x1
11. 2x1
12. 2x4
13. 2x10
A only
14. 10x1
15. 1x8
16. 4x10
17. 7x9
18. 9x7
19. 10x3
20. 2x9
21. 3x9
22. 6x1
23. 2x5
24. 4x6
25. 10x8
26. 3x2
27. 1x3
28. 6x10
P/1st=2nd
29. 9x8
30. 1x4
31. 3x6
32. 10x2

33. 6x2
34. 6x9
35. 3x3
A only
36. 5x6
37. 8x0
38. 5x5
39. 5x1
40. 10x9
41. 3x7
42. 7x10
43. 8x4
44. 10x5
45. 2x8
46. 9x6
47. 3x1
P/1st=2nd
48. 4x1
49. 7x2
50. 8x10
51. 6x4
52. 8x7
53. 8x2
54. 1x6
55. 7x6
56. 4x4
57. 9x0
58. 10x6
59. 5x2
60. 3x0
A only
61. 5x0
62. 8x3
63. 7x3
64. 9x9
65. 9x2

66. 10x7
67. 3x10
68. 6x0
P/1st=2nd
69. 10x0
70. 5x4
71. 1x1
72. 7x8
73. 6x3
74. 6x7
75. 1x9
76. 3x8
77. 2x3
78. 9x5
79. 9x4
A only
80. 5x3
81. 7x4
82. 8x6
83. 9x10
84. 2x0
85. 1x7
86. 6x8
87. 3x5
88. 9x3
89. 4x5
P/1st=2nd
90. 5x8
91. 6x6
92. 1x0
93. 10x10
94. 7x5
95. 8x9
96. 8x8
97. 9x1
98. 5x7

99. 1x5
100. 2x7

All Multiplication Facts, Set 7

P/1st=2nd
1. 9x4
2. 4x0
3. 5x2
4. 5x7
5. 2x6
6. 6x10
7. 8x1
8. 3x6
9. 7x8
10. 3x1
A only
11. 10x6
12. 10x10
13. 5x8
14. 5x3
15. 3x3
16. 1x2
17. 7x9
18. 6x2
19. 1x0
20. 3x9
21. 6x4
P/1st=2nd
22. 1x5
23. 3x2
24. 9x0
25. 8x8
26. 2x2
27. 9x5
28. 3x5
29. 5x6
A only
30. 8x4
31. 5x10
32. 6x1

33. 2x0
34. 2x3
35. 6x7
36. 9x1
37. 7x3
38. 10x4
39. 10x7
40. 8x2
P/1st=2nd
41. 8x9
42. 3x10
43. 4x9
44. 8x10
45. 5x0
46. 7x4
47. 7x6
48. 7x5
49. 7x1
50. 4x2
51. 4x6
52. 1x10
A only
53. 7x7
54. 6x5
55. 10x8
56. 2x9
57. 6x9
58. 1x1
59. 2x7
60. 2x5
61. 9x10
62. 5x4
63. 3x8
64. 6x8
65. 4x5
P/1st=2nd

66. 2x4
67. 9x2
68. 9x6
69. 3x4
70. 6x6
71. 5x1
72. 4x7
73. 4x8
74. 7x10
75. 7x0
76. 9x3
77. 10x2
78. 2x8
79. 1x3
80. 10x5
A only
81. 8x0
82. 1x4
83. 10x1
84. 3x7
85. 8x6
86. 1x7
87. 5x9
P/1st=2nd
88. 5x5
89. 10x0
90. 6x0
91. 8x3
92. 1x6
A only
93. 2x10
94. 9x9
95. 1x8
96. 10x3
97. 4x10
98. 8x5

99. 4x3
100. 9x7

All Multiplication Facts, Set 8

Num and A
1. 7x3
2. 8x10
3. 9x0
4. 3x1
5. 7x1
6. 1x2
7. 4x4
8. 2x2
9. 8x8
10. 10x0
11. 4x3
P/1st=2nd
12. 4x2
13. 9x5
14. 1x4
15. 6x2
16. 3x9
17. 5x3
18. 2x0
19. 8x3
20. 5x7
21. 9x10
22. 5x10
23. 10x9
Num and A
24. 4x1
25. 1x3
26. 6x8
27. 1x9
28. 1x7
29. 3x0
30. 5x8
31. 7x0
32. 2x6
33. 6x0

34. 4x8
P/1st=2nd
35. 10x2
36. 3x2
37. 2x8
38. 3x10
39. 6x6
40. 4x9
41. 10x10
42. 10x6
43. 2x10
44. 4x6
Num and A
45. 4x0
46. 3x5
47. 8x9
48. 9x2
49. 10x7
50. 7x9
51. 3x7
P/1st=2nd
52. 9x4
53. 4x5
54. 8x4
55. 7x7
56. 6x3
57. 8x1
58. 10x4
59. 7x8
60. 7x4
61. 2x3
62. 6x7
63. 2x7
64. 9x1
65. 8x0
66. 10x3

Num and A
67. 5x5
68. 10x5
69. 6x10
70. 8x2
71. 3x4
72. 1x0
73. 6x1
74. 9x9
75. 8x5
76. 4x10
77. 6x4
78. 7x10
79. 3x8
P/1st=2nd
80. 7x6
81. 6x9
82. 3x3
83. 3x6
84. 9x7
Num and A
85. 2x4
86. 9x6
87. 9x8
88. 7x2
89. 5x9
90. 5x6
91. 2x9
92. 5x2
P/1st=2nd
93. 10x1
94. 5x4
95. 10x8
96. 8x6
97. 2x1
98. 7x5

99. 9x3
100. 1x1

Division Facts

All Division Facts, Set 1

A only
1. 28/7
2. 4/4
3. 36/6
4. 5/1
5. 15/3
6. 20/4
7. 56/7
8. 0/2

Num and A
9. 42/7
10. 63/7
11. 6/1
12. 45/9
13. 8/8
14. 50/10
15. 90/9
16. 45/5
17. 0/3
18. 63/9
19. 30/10

A only
20. 6/6
21. 18/9
22. 72/9
23. 6/3
24. 16/4
25. 16/8
26. 60/6
27. 30/3
28. 24/6
29. 14/2
30. 0/4
31. 36/4

Num and A
32. 24/4
33. 35/5
34. 20/2
35. 0/6
36. 40/10
37. 80/8
38. 16/2
39. 30/6
40. 0/7
41. 42/6
42. 70/10
43. 5/5
44. 54/6

A only
45. 9/3
46. 72/8
47. 12/4
48. 32/8
49. 24/3
50. 28/4
51. 4/2
52. 36/9
53. 90/10
54. 40/8
55. 24/8
56. 80/10
57. 100/10
58. 3/1
59. 81/9

Num and A
60. 21/7
61. 20/10
62. 2/2

63. 70/7
64. 64/8
65. 0/1
66. 12/3
67. 32/4

A only
68. 6/2
69. 27/9
70. 30/5
71. 50/5
72. 49/7
73. 48/8
74. 14/7
75. 18/3
76. 2/1
77. 15/5

Num and A
78. 8/2
79. 0/5
80. 7/1
81. 12/2
82. 35/7
83. 40/4
84. 18/2
85. 8/1
86. 56/8
87. 25/5
88. 10/10

A only
89. 0/9
90. 0/8
91. 9/1
92. 1/1
93. 48/6

94. 60/10
95. 18/6

Num and A
96. 4/1
97. 3/3
98. 20/5
99. 9/9
100. 10/5

All Division Facts, Set 2

Q and A
1. 7/1
2. 5/5
3. 36/4
4. 80/8
5. 0/7
6. 21/7
7. 1/1
8. 2/2
9. 8/2
10. 35/5
11. 45/5
A only
12. 40/5
13. 18/9
14. 27/9
15. 50/5
16. 100/10
17. 15/3
18. 9/9
19. 9/1
20. 16/8
21. 12/6
22. 28/7
23. 0/6
24. 54/6
25. 72/8
26. 20/4
Q and A
27. 18/3
28. 35/7
29. 32/8
30. 10/2
31. 0/2
32. 14/7
33. 30/6

34. 12/4
A only
35. 36/9
36. 70/10
37. 0/10
38. 49/7
39. 3/1
40. 0/5
41. 40/4
42. 28/4
43. 70/7
44. 4/4
45. 36/6
46. 90/9
Q and A
47. 48/6
48. 8/8
49. 24/8
50. 4/2
51. 9/3
52. 0/1
53. 20/5
54. 6/1
55. 40/10
56. 72/9
57. 50/10
A only
58. 21/3
59. 90/10
60. 10/1
61. 54/9
62. 42/6
Q and A
63. 8/1
64. 24/6
65. 56/7

66. 4/1
67. 60/10
68. 20/10
69. 12/2
70. 0/9
71. 2/1
72. 6/3
73. 42/7
74. 7/7
75. 63/9
A only
76. 8/4
77. 10/10
78. 27/3
79. 10/5
80. 63/7
81. 30/5
82. 14/2
83. 18/2
84. 0/4
85. 15/5
Q and A
86. 60/6
87. 24/3
88. 16/2
89. 12/3
90. 25/5
91. 45/9
92. 24/4
A only
93. 30/10
94. 3/3
95. 64/8
96. 56/8
97. 40/8
98. 48/8

99. 30/3
100. 0/3

All Division Facts, Set 3

A only
1. 50/10
2. 72/8
3. 8/1
4. 40/4
5. 6/6
6. 15/3
7. 40/8
8. 10/5
9. 6/3
10. 81/9
11. 0/4
12. 60/10
Num and A
13. 8/2
14. 2/2
15. 3/1
16. 0/10
17. 7/7
18. 9/3
19. 63/7
20. 40/5
21. 80/10
22. 90/9
23. 70/10
A only
24. 30/5
25. 0/7
26. 28/7
27. 30/6
28. 20/4
Num and A
29. 5/1
30. 25/5
31. 5/5
32. 6/1

33. 45/5
34. 48/6
35. 9/9
36. 12/6
37. 36/4
38. 12/2
39. 40/10
40. 36/9
41. 42/6
A only
42. 0/5
43. 8/4
44. 18/6
45. 24/6
46. 90/10
47. 80/8
48. 42/7
49. 30/10
50. 48/8
51. 20/5
Num and A
52. 24/8
53. 16/4
54. 4/2
55. 21/7
56. 3/3
57. 12/4
58. 50/5
A only
59. 35/5
60. 0/1
61. 16/8
62. 49/7
63. 36/6
64. 27/9
65. 1/1

66. 32/4
67. 20/2
68. 64/8
69. 54/9
70. 12/3
71. 72/9
72. 56/7
73. 35/7
Num and A
74. 70/7
75. 14/7
76. 45/9
77. 10/2
78. 20/10
79. 18/3
80. 6/2
81. 9/1
82. 10/1
83. 0/8
84. 60/6
A only
85. 27/3
86. 15/5
87. 8/8
88. 10/10
89. 100/10
90. 0/9
91. 0/2
92. 16/2
Num and A
93. 30/3
94. 28/4
95. 32/8
96. 4/4
97. 4/1
98. 7/1

99. 18/2
100. 21/3

All Division Facts, Set 4

Q and A
1. 20/5
2. 25/5
3. 6/6
4. 4/1
5. 2/1
6. 20/2
7. 60/10
8. 45/5
9. 24/4
10. 30/10
11. 2/2
12. 0/1
13. 60/6
14. 14/7
15. 5/1

A only
16. 36/4
17. 28/4
18. 18/6
19. 16/2
20. 28/7
21. 0/6
22. 56/8
23. 0/10
24. 100/10
25. 72/8
26. 10/5

Q and A
27. 24/8
28. 70/10
29. 8/2
30. 4/2
31. 18/3
32. 20/4
33. 3/3

34. 90/10

A only
35. 30/3
36. 6/1
37. 0/9
38. 18/9
39. 14/2
40. 54/6
41. 16/8

Q and A
42. 8/8
43. 35/7
44. 36/6
45. 0/3
46. 27/3
47. 10/2
48. 40/5
49. 30/6
50. 42/6
51. 64/8

A only
52. 48/6
53. 36/9
54. 21/3
55. 40/10
56. 0/2
57. 56/7
58. 24/3
59. 15/3
60. 80/10
61. 6/3
62. 40/8

Q and A
63. 90/9
64. 50/10
65. 6/2

66. 50/5
67. 30/5

A only
68. 24/6
69. 18/2
70. 70/7
71. 5/5
72. 9/9
73. 12/3
74. 10/1
75. 9/3
76. 40/4
77. 27/9
78. 63/7
79. 0/8
80. 80/8

Q and A
81. 7/1
82. 10/10
83. 8/4
84. 1/1
85. 12/6
86. 4/4
87. 12/4
88. 72/9
89. 7/7
90. 9/1
91. 12/2
92. 81/9

A only
93. 35/5
94. 42/7
95. 48/8
96. 16/4
97. 21/7
98. 8/1

99. 0/4
100. 45/9

All Division Facts, Set 5

Num and A
1. 14/7
2. 18/9
3. 18/3
4. 42/6
5. 40/10
6. 6/2
7. 24/4
8. 24/3
A only
9. 7/7
10. 9/3
11. 54/9
12. 32/4
13. 8/4
14. 54/6
15. 10/10
16. 18/6
17. 63/9
18. 8/1
19. 24/8
20. 56/8
Num and A
21. 30/6
22. 0/1
23. 15/3
24. 2/1
25. 80/8
26. 28/7
27. 25/5
28. 10/1
29. 4/2
30. 45/9
31. 50/10
32. 9/9
33. 0/8

A only
34. 81/9
35. 50/5
36. 6/1
37. 12/4
38. 10/2
39. 30/10
40. 16/8
41. 70/10
42. 1/1
43. 40/5
44. 63/7
45. 48/8
46. 14/2
47. 5/1
48. 24/6
Num and A
49. 35/7
50. 7/1
51. 3/1
52. 27/3
53. 80/10
54. 45/5
55. 30/5
56. 36/6
57. 48/6
58. 4/4
59. 20/10
A only
60. 60/6
61. 30/3
62. 16/4
63. 27/9
64. 60/10
65. 56/7
66. 49/7

67. 0/4
Num and A
68. 20/4
69. 0/3
70. 6/6
71. 8/8
72. 12/3
73. 5/5
74. 18/2
A only
75. 21/7
76. 3/3
77. 40/4
78. 2/2
79. 100/10
Num and A
80. 20/2
81. 40/8
82. 70/7
83. 36/9
84. 36/4
85. 90/10
86. 42/7
87. 0/10
88. 12/6
89. 16/2
90. 72/9
A only
91. 28/4
92. 0/7
93. 12/2
94. 32/8
95. 8/2
96. 0/9
97. 90/9
98. 10/5

99. 72/8
100. 4/1

Task-Switching with All 4 Operations

All 4 Operations, Set 1

Q and A
1. 6/1
2. 56/8
3. 24/6
4. 2/1
5. 13-6
6. 5+2
7. 1x9
A only
8. 7+4
9. 3-1
10. 10+0
11. 6-0
12. 28/7
13. 8+9
14. 3+9
15. 12-4
16. 1/1
Q and A
17. 35/5
18. 9-7
19. 5x3
20. 7x0
21. 7x3
A only
22. 7x7
23. 8x1
24. 45/9
25. 8+10
26. 4x2
27. 5/1
28. 8x5
29. 80/8
30. 54/6

31. 6x0
Q and A
32. 9/3
33. 9+7
34. 2+7
35. 6+6
36. 49/7
37. 3+10
38. 8x8
39. 45/5
40. 2+5
41. 7+3
A only
42. 3+0
43. 6-1
44. 4x10
45. 17-9
46. 5x2
47. 0+1
48. 2+2
49. 8+4
50. 0/8
51. 0+8
Q and A
52. 4x1
53. 4-0
54. 4+5
55. 16-6
56. 8/1
57. 10-5
58. 2+3
59. 30/5
60. 72/8
61. 15/5

62. 0x8
A only
63. 4-2
64. 4+3
65. 2+10
66. 11-9
67. 14-10
68. 4/1
69. 18/3
70. 16-10
71. 4/4
Q and A
72. 14-4
73. 9+0
74. 0x10
75. 9x10
76. 3+3
A only
77. 27/3
78. 1+4
79. 8-0
80. 2x10
81. 10-6
82. 3+2
83. 3x4
84. 7-1
85. 18/2
86. 40/5
Q and A
87. 5x9
88. 50/5
89. 7x5
90. 5x6
91. 5x10

92. 8x7
A only
93. 8+3
94. 6+9
Q and A
95. 7x9
96. 9x4
97. 3/3
98. 10x0
99. 56/7
100. 6x5

All 4 Operations, Set 2

Num and A
1. 24/3
2. 2x8
3. 13-3
4. 8x6
5. 17-8
6. 25/5
7. 15-6
8. 3x10

A only
9. 8-7
10. 1+6
11. 0+2
12. 8-5
13. 11-4

Num and A
14. 16/4
15. 7+9
16. 5-2
17. 20/5
18. 7x4
19. 48/6
20. 5/5
21. 17-10
22. 10x5

A only
23. 9-6
24. 7+7
25. 0x2
26. 2+4
27. 6-2
28. 0/5
29. 6+4
30. 12-5
31. 12-10
32. 11-7

33. 3+1
Num and A
34. 18-9
35. 6-4
36. 7+5
37. 4/2

A only
38. 8/4
39. 2-0
40. 10-3
41. 15-9
42. 3+4
43. 7+6
44. 8-1
45. 0x9
46. 6/6
47. 3x6

Num and A
48. 7-2
49. 3-2
50. 4x3
51. 11-5
52. 9+3
53. 32/4
54. 4x9
55. 0/10
56. 18/6
57. 20/2
58. 10+10

A only
59. 15-10
60. 4-1
61. 0/9
62. 10/5
63. 18/9
64. 6+2

65. 8x10
66. 9+1
Num and A
67. 13-8
68. 6+1
69. 1x7
70. 4x5
71. 5-0
72. 10x10
73. 5x1
74. 9x5
75. 32/8

A only
76. 5+6
77. 6x8
78. 7-0
79. 12/4
80. 6x4
81. 12-9

Num and A
82. 8-8
83. 12/6
84. 9+2
85. 0+6
86. 7-7

A only
87. 10x3
88. 7x8
89. 8+7
90. 17-7
91. 8+5
92. 2/2
93. 30/6

Num and A
94. 5x4
95. 14-7

96. 14-6
97. 9-2
A only
98. 9/1
99. 5+3
100. 12-2

All 4 Operations, Set 3

A only
1. 9x0
2. 10x4
3. 7-3
4. 6x2
5. 48/8
6. 14-5
7. 1+5
8. 6+7
9. 2+0
10. 36/4
11. 0x7

Q and A
12. 1x6
13. 4+10
14. 15-7
15. 14-9
16. 15-5
17. 13-4
18. 5x5
19. 4x6
20. 3+5

A only
21. 9+9
22. 7x6
23. 54/9
24. 9-1
25. 2+6
26. 2x6
27. 13-5
28. 4x8
29. 5-3

Q and A
30. 10-9
31. 3+6
32. 0/6

33. 3-3
34. 1+2
35. 9/9
36. 5+10
37. 6x1
38. 2x9
39. 9+10

A only
40. 10+1
41. 14-8
42. 3x0
43. 7/1
44. 2x1
45. 10+3
46. 11-1
47. 1x1
48. 10+5
49. 1x0

Q and A
50. 11-6
51. 5+1
52. 13-9
53. 0x0
54. 5x8
55. 28/4

A only
56. 12-3
57. 6x6
58. 8+2
59. 6/3
60. 4+4
61. 2x5
62. 8-6
63. 0/4
64. 0x1
65. 8x4

Q and A
66. 27/9
67. 5-1
68. 9x9
69. 18-8
70. 0+7
71. 15/3
72. 10-1
73. 10-8
74. 72/9
75. 6x10
76. 1-0
77. 10-7
78. 11-3
79. 36/6

A only
80. 7-6
81. 7x1
82. 24/4
83. 5x7
84. 9x8

Q and A
85. 3x2
86. 3x3
87. 9-0
88. 9x6
89. 6x9
90. 16/8

A only
91. 9-9
92. 13-10
93. 9+5
94. 8+8
95. 8-3

Q and A
96. 7-4

97. 1-1
98. 10+9
99. 4+9
100. 6/2

All 4 Operations, Set 4

A only
1. 6-6
2. 10x7
3. 2x3
4. 10+7
Num and A
5. 8/2
6. 2x7
7. 6+0
8. 1x2
9. 0/1
10. 1+8
11. 0+5
12. 5+8
13. 0+0
14. 9x1
A only
15. 8x3
16. 9x7
17. 9-4
18. 6-3
19. 2-1
20. 16-8
21. 10+8
22. 5+0
23. 6x3
24. 12-7
25. 10+2
26. 16-7
Num and A
27. 40/4
28. 6+5
29. 4+8
30. 6+8
31. 2+1
32. 6x7

33. 5x0
A only
34. 10-4
35. 0+9
36. 10-2
37. 12/2
38. 16/2
39. 60/6
40. 7+8
41. 4-4
42. 21/3
43. 19-10
44. 8x2
45. 4+2
46. 1+10
47. 1+3
Num and A
48. 2+9
49. 2x2
50. 11-8
51. 0/7
52. 9+6
53. 9-8
54. 4+0
A only
55. 9-5
56. 1+7
57. 2x0
58. 11-2
59. 5+4
Num and A
60. 2-2
61. 4+7
62. 5+9
63. 5+7
64. 10+6

65. 4x0
66. 8-4
67. 3x8
68. 7x2
69. 10x9
A only
70. 10+4
71. 19-9
72. 3x5
73. 6+3
74. 0-0
75. 42/6
76. 3/1
77. 8-2
Num and A
78. 6+10
79. 9-3
80. 7+2
81. 3x7
82. 7/7
A only
83. 63/7
84. 0/3
Num and A
85. 8+0
86. 11-10
87. 12-8
88. 9x2
89. 8+1
90. 0x6
91. 3x9
92. 36/9
93. 7+1
A only
94. 4+1
95. 10/2

96. 9+4
97. 0/2
98. 7x10
Num and A
99. 20/4
100. 8/8

All 4 Operations, Set 5

Q and A
1. 70/7
2. 3+8
3. 5+5
4. 40/8
5. 1+9
6. 0x5

A only
7. 7-5
8. 8x9
9. 0+3
10. 10-10
11. 1x4
12. 4x7
13. 0+4
14. 1x3

Q and A
15. 18-10
16. 14/7
17. 12/3
18. 16-9
19. 4-3
20. 42/7
21. 1x5
22. 4x4
23. 1x8
24. 35/7

A only
25. 10x6
26. 7+10
27. 5-5
28. 24/8
29. 6-5
30. 81/9
31. 15-8

32. 0x4
33. 20-10

Q and A
34. 30/3
35. 12-6
36. 3+7
37. 9+8
38. 3-0
39. 10x2
40. 3x1
41. 10/1
42. 10x8
43. 0x3
44. 9x3

A only
45. 1+0
46. 13-7
47. 5-4
48. 8+6

Q and A
49. 63/9
50. 1+1
51. 14/2
52. 21/7
53. 2x4
54. 10-0
55. 2+8

A only
56. 8x0
57. 64/8
58. 4+6
59. 7+0
60. 90/9
61. 4x2
62. 5x9

63. 7x3
64. 10-5
65. 5x1
66. 7/7

Q and A
67. 19-10
68. 5+5
69. 12-10
70. 10+5
71. 7x10
72. 9+3
73. 0x4
74. 49/7

A only
75. 10+9
76. 6+9
77. 0/3
78. 56/7
79. 16-8
80. 7x5

Q and A
81. 9+1
82. 2x3
83. 9x7
84. 1-0

A only
85. 9+2
86. 2x0
87. 20/5
88. 2+9
89. 3+7
90. 12-7
91. 4x9
92. 11-10
93. 5/1

94. 3+6
95. 0+6
96. 11-6

Q and A
97. 4+4
98. 7-6
99. 2+5
100. 13-10

Math Word Problems

Word Problems Involving Addition and Subtraction

First, go through these problems until you understand them all. Then you can do task-switching between "A only" (where you say the number that is the solution to the problem) and "Which Op" (where you say which operation is necessary to find the answer – is it addition or subtraction?

For example, suppose the stimulus is, "There are three crows on a fence. Two fly away. How many are left?" The response using "A only" is "1." The response using "Which Op" is "subtract."

A only:

1. Jim has 3 books, and buys 2 more. How many does he own after buying?

2. Fran has 7 books, and sells 4. How many does she own after selling?

3. A puppy is 9 inches long, and grows 2 inches. How many inches tall is he after growing?

4. A plant is 10 centimeters tall, and grows 4 centimeters. How tall is it after growing?

5. Jim has 8 dollars, and earns 2 dollars more. How much does he have after earning?

Which op

6. Fran has 9 dollars, and spends 3 dollars. How much does she have after spending?

7. There are 8 windows. 3 get broken. How many windows remain unbroken?

8. There are 5 bugs in the room. 2 more fly in. How many are in the room now?

9. There are 8 sacks of sand. We get 3 more. How many do we have after getting those?

A only

10. We have 11 pencils. Two get used up. How many do we have left?

11. It's 10 kilometers to town from where we are. We go 6 kilometers toward town. How many kilometers from town are we now?

12. John owes $14 to Tim. John pays $9 back. How much does he owe Tim after that repaying?

13. Jim is 10 kilometers north of town. He goes 3 kilometers farther north. How far north of town is he now?

14. Jan is 8 kilometers north of town. She goes 2 kilometers south (towards town). How far north of town is she now?

15. Al has read 10 pages of a book. He reads 7 more pages. How many has he read altogether?

16. Min has 9 pages to read. She reads 4 pages. How many pages are left to read?

17. There are 6 bugs in the room. 3 fly out. How many are left?

18. Sal wants to save $10. She saves $3. How many dollars are left for her to save?

19. Ralph goes 5 miles east from his home. Then he goes 5 more miles east. How many miles east of home is he now?

20. A rope is 10 meters long. 2 meters are cut off. How many meters are left?

21. A chain is 4 meters long. It's joined end to end with another chain 7 meters long. How long is the resulting chain?

Which op

22. Ralph is 10 years old. Sue is 7 years old. How much older is Ralph than Sue?

23. Jim has $8. Tina has $9. How much do they have altogether?

24. Sarah's lunch bill is $10. Sarah leaves a tip of $2. How much does Sarah spend on lunch altogether?

25. A book costs 30 dollars before tax. The tax is 2 dollars. How much does the book cost in all?

26. The original price of a book is 10 dollars. Because of a sale, the price is reduced 2 dollars. What's the new price of the book?

27. John owes Tim $3. Then John borrows $4 more. Now how much does John owe Tim?

28. Paul owes his mom $10. Then he pays back $4. How much does he owe her now?

A only

29. Jay is 5 feet tall. Lisa is 3 feet tall. How much taller is Jay than Lisa?

30. A hole is 2 meters deep. We dig down 2 more meters. How deep is the hole now?

31. A jug holds 6 liters of water. We drink 4 liters. How much water is left?

32. Alex weighs 100 pounds. He gains 10 pounds. How much does he weigh after gaining?

33. John types 9 pages on Monday, and 7 pages on Tuesday. How many pages did he type over the two days?

Which op

34. A pancake is 100 calories, and the syrup on it is 100 more calories. How many calories altogether are in the pancake and syrup?

35. I have $13, and I spend $6. How much do I have left?

36. I go 10 meters north of my starting point, and then come back 8 meters straight south. How far am I from my starting point?

37. Jed can run 12 kilometers per hour, and Rod can run 8 kilometers per hour. How much faster than Rod can Jed run?

38. Tom weighs 50 pounds and his little brother weighs 20 pounds. When Tom holds his little brother and they both get on the scale, what's their combined weight?

39. Gina weighs 100 pounds. She loses 10 pounds. How much does she weigh after losing?

A only

40. Jacob has 10 friends. He makes 3 more friends. How many friends does he have after making the new ones?

41. Bert gets on the scale, and it reads 100 pounds. He takes 1 pound of stuff out of his pocket, and puts it on a table. What's the scale reading now?

42. Jean has 10 friends who live in her town. 3 of them move away. Now how many friends does she have in her town?

43. A shirt originally costs 17 dollars. There is a discount of 8 dollars. How much does the shirt cost after the discount?

44. A merchant buys a shirt for 10 dollars. He marks the shirt up by 5 dollars. How much does he sell the shirt for?

45. The runner who finishes a race first, finishes in 9 minutes. The second place runner has a time of 11 minutes. How many minutes went by between the winner's finish and the second placer's finish?

46. A mixture has 8 kilograms of water and 5 kilograms of alcohol (and none of anything else). How many kilograms in the mixture altogether?

Which op

47. There are 9 pounds of salt water. 1 pound of the mixture is salt. How much of the mixture is water?

48. Ted sleeps 7 hours at night, and later takes a 2 hour nap. How many hours has he slept altogether?

49. One pill has 10 milligrams of medicine, and another has 5 milligrams. How many milligrams does someone get by taking both pills together?

50. Someone wants to take 20 milligrams of medicine. The person has already taken 10 milligrams. How many milligrams more should the person take?

51. There are 10 questions on a test, all of which Jane gets either right or wrong. She gets 9 right. How many did she miss?

52. On a test, Frank answered all the questions and got 9 right and 3 wrong. How many questions were on the test?

53. The contents of John's suitcase weigh 10 pounds and the suitcase itself weighs 2 pounds. How much does the suitcase weigh with the contents in it?

54. A suitcase with a bunch of stuff in it weighs 10 pounds. The stuff by itself weighs 7 pounds. How much does the suitcase weigh?

55. Three weights, altogether, weigh 8 pounds. The first two, together, weigh 6 pounds. How much does the third one weigh?

56. Three weights, together, weigh 9 pounds. A fourth weight weighs

7 pounds. How much do all four of them weigh altogether?

A only

57. Three people have, altogether, $8. A fourth person has $4. How much do all four people have?

58. Five people have, altogether, $7. When a sixth person pools her money with the first five, the six people altogether have $15. How much money did the sixth person have?

59. Sunny can do 25 math facts per minute. She increases her speed by 10 facts per minute. How fast can she go after increasing her speed?

60. Harold knows how to play 14 songs. He forgets how to play 8 of them. How many does he know how to play after forgetting?

61. Gina counts some baby pigs. She gets a total of 10. Gina's mom correctly says, "There were two pigs that you counted twice." How many baby pigs were really there?

62. Tommy counts some baby pigs. He gets a total of 6. Tommy's dad correctly says, "There was one you missed who was hiding behind a tree." How many baby pigs were really there?

63. Rick wants to buy something for $12. He has $7. How many more dollars does he need to get?

64. Tonya gets paid $17 per hour. Lisa gets paid $10 per hour. How much more, per hour, does Tonya get paid than Lisa?

65. Tonya gets paid $17 per hour, and Lisa gets paid $10 per hour. If they pool their money, how much do they make each hour, altogether?

66. All 10 members of a group study Spanish. 2 of them study both Spanish and French. How many of them study Spanish and not French?

Which op

67. Kristy has to wait 10 minutes for a play to start. After she waits 6 minutes, how much longer does she have to wait?

68. Larry thinks a play will start in 10 minutes after he sits down. But after he waits that long, the play doesn't start for 7 more minutes. How long did Larry sit waiting altogether?

69. A person spends 5 dollars on food and 8 dollars on presents. How much did the person spend altogether?

70. A person spends 15 dollars altogether. 10 dollars of that were spent on food. How much was spent on something other than food?

71. 3 people ride in one car, and 6 people ride in a van. How many people travel altogether, in the two vehicles?

A only

72. 14 people go from one building to another. 6 of them rode bicycles. How many of them went by some means other than bicycle?

73. A snake is 18 inches long after growing 8 inches. How long was the snake before she grew the 8 inches?

74. Gina's first name has 4 letters, and her last name has 9 letters. How many letters total are in her first and last name?

75. Gina's first name has 4 letters, and her last name has 9 letters. How many more letters are in her last name than in her first?

76. Sara is 10 years old, and Tim is 6 years old. How many years older than Tim is Sara?

77. An old broken computer is on sale for 17 dollars. Another one is on sale for 9 dollars. How much more does the first cost than the second?

78. Lottie started high school when she was 14 years old. She started college 4 years later. How old was she when she started college?

Which op

79. Everyone in a certain high school studies either Spanish or French, but not both. In a group of 15 students, 9 of them study Spanish. How many study French?

80. A group of 17 students has 9 males. How many females are in the group?

81. There are 7 males and 9 females in a group. How many people are in the group in all?

82. A window sill is 2 feet higher than the floor. The top of the window is 4 feet higher than the window sill. How far above the floor is the top of the window?

83. A window sill is 2 feet higher than the floor. The top of a window is 7 feet higher than the floor. How far is it from the windowsill to the top of the window?

84. A room is 9 feet from floor to ceiling. A cabinet is 6 feet tall. How many feet are there from the top of the cabinet to the ceiling?

85. There are 9 boxes of stuff to move from the bedroom, and 8 boxes to move from the office. How many boxes are there to move, from the two rooms combined?

86. The temperature was 40 degrees at 2 pm, and 30 degrees at 9 pm. By how many degrees did the temperature drop?

87. One appliance uses 100 watts of power, and another uses 200 watts. How much power do they use when both are turned on?

88. John wants to take 16 credits of college courses. He is signed up for 9 credits already. How many more credits does he need to sign up for?

89. Tom buys a 3 acre lot, right next to his 4 acre property. How big

is his property altogether after the purchase?

90. Richard owns 15 acres of land, but he sells a lot that is 8 acres. How much land does he own after the sale?

A only

91. A merchant buys a computer for 200 dollars and sells it for 300 dollars. What is the merchant's profit?

92. A merchant buys a computer for 300 dollars. He wants to make 200 dollars profit when selling it. For how much should he list the price of it?

93. A merchant lists the price of a computer as 600 dollars. He advertises a sale with a 100 dollar discount taken off the list price. What is the sale price?

94. Someone has a 10 page paper to write. The person has written 2 pages. How many more pages are there to write?

Which op

95. Someone is writing a paper. The person writes 5 pages in the morning, and 3 in the afternoon. How many pages has the person

written in both morning and afternoon?

96. A person runs 100 meters in 18 seconds. He wants to improve his speed by 4 seconds. If he succeeds, what will be his new time for the 100 meter run?

97. A person runs 100 meters in 20 seconds. He doesn't exercise, gets more out of shape, and gets slower by 4 seconds. What is his time after getting out of shape?

98. A person can lift 100 pounds. He gets stronger, so that he can lift 10 pounds more. How much can he lift after getting stronger?

99. A person can lift 100 pounds. He gets weaker by 10 pounds. How much can he lift after getting weaker?

100.   A person leases an office for 2 years. After a few months, he decides he likes the office so much that he wants to extend the original lease by 3 more years. How long is the period of the lease after he extends it?

Word Problems Involving All 4 Operations

A only:

1. There are 3 rooms, and 4 people in each room. How many people in all?

2. There are 18 peanuts, distributed equally among 3 bags. How many in each bag?

3. 15 cards are dealt equally to 5 people. How many cards does each get?

4. A rectangle is 7 centimeters long and 5 centimeters wide. What is its area, in square centimeters?

5. Someone has 18 dollars and spends 9 dollars. How much is left?

6. Someone walks 3 km east of a starting point, and then goes 7 km further east. Now how far east of the starting point is the person?

7. Someone has 20 dollars. How many things can he buy, if each thing costs 5 dollars?

8. Each of 4 spiders has 8 legs. How many legs are there in all?

9. Someone has 8 nickels, each of which is worth 5 cents. How much are the coins worth in all?

10. In the year 2008, someone was 8 years old. What year was the person born in?

11. The area of a rectangle is 36 square centimeters. The length is 9 centimeters. What is the width?

Which op

12. Someone goes 7 miles each hour, for 3 hours. How many miles does the person go in all?

13. Someone wants to go 24 kilometers. The person walks at 4 km per hour. How long does it take the person?

14. Each of 4 people has 7 dollars. How many dollars do they have in all?

15. 6 people are each pushing against a car with a force of 50 pounds. How much force are they pushing with altogether?

16. Someone wants to each no more than 50 calories from cherries. Each cherry is 5 calories. How

80

many cherries can the person eat?

17. Someone eats two grapes which together provide 4 calories, and a bite of tomato which is 3 calories. How many has the person eaten in all?

18. Someone eats 6 cherries, which are 5 calories apiece. How many calories has the person taken in, in all?

19. Someone wants to eat a maximum of 3000 calories in a day. The person has eaten 2000 calories. How many more calories can the person eat?

20. 6 weights each weigh 4 pounds. How much do they weigh if you put them all on a scale at once?

21. Marvin earns 10 dollars an hour. How much does he earn in 7 hours?

22. Marvin earns 10 dollars an hour. How long will it take for him to earn 40 dollars?

23. Sally is working a shift that is 10 hours long. She has worked 6 hours. How many hours does she have before she gets off work?

24. Each of 9 mother rabbits has 6 baby rabbits. How many baby rabbits were born?

25. Each of 8 insects has 6 legs. How many legs are there in all?

26. A bunch of insects, each of which has 6 legs, has 36 legs altogether. How many insects are there?

A only

27. Each of 7 boxes has mass of 4 kilograms. How much mass do the boxes have altogether?

28. 8 identical boxes have a total mass of 56 kilograms. How much mass is there in each box?

29. Each person in a group has 10 fingers. There are 90 fingers in all. How many people are there?

30. John buys a lunch for 9 people at 7 dollars apiece. How much does he spend in all?

31. Sally pays 72 dollars for lunches for 8 people. How much did each lunch cost?

32. 10 identical computers, when put on a scale, weigh 100 pounds. How much does each computer weigh?

33. It takes Maria 20 minutes to give a dog a haircut. How many minutes will it take her to give haircuts to 4 dogs?

34. Each trip across the college is 2 kilometers. How far does someone go in 8 trips across the college?

Which op

35. A truck goes 10 miles for each gallon of gas. How far can the truck go on 8 gallons of gas?

36. A truck goes 10 miles for each gallon of gas. How many gallons will it take for the truck to go 50 miles?

37. Joe gets a haircut 10 times a year. Each one costs $5. How much does he spend in all on haircuts in a year?

38. Fran bought 8 cans of vegetables, at the same price. The vegetables cost her 8 dollars altogether. How much did each can of vegetables cost?

39. One can of vegetables cost 40 cents and another cost 30 cents. How much did they cost in all?

40. Tina has an assignment to read 17 pages. She has read 7 pages. How many more does she have to read?

41. It is now 6 minutes after 8. A concert begins at 10 minutes after 8. How many minutes is it until the concert begins?

42. Mack waits 2 minutes each time he turns his computer on, once each day. How many minutes, total, does he wait for the computer to come on in a month which is 30 days long?

43. There are 7 days in a week. Rhonda is getting married in exactly 6 weeks. How many days will it be before she gets married?

44. People have allotted 56 total minutes for speeches. Each speaker gets the same amount of time. There are 7 speakers. How long does each get to speak?

45. There are 80 pounds of books to be moved. Each of 8 people gets an equal amount of the weight. How much weight does each person carry?

46. Tom sleeps two hours a night more than Gary does. In 7 days, how much more sleep, total, does Tom get than Gary?

A only

47. In one night, Jean sleeps 9 hours and Tonya sleeps 6 hours. How many more hours sleep did Jean get than Tonya?

48. The temperature is 8 degrees Celsius, and then the temperature rises 7 degrees. What's the temperature after the increase?

49. John has 3 nephews graduating from school, and he gives each of them a 50 dollar present. How much does John give in all?

50. Terry has 20 dollars to spend on books. Each book costs 4 dollars. How many books can she buy?

51. There are 63 pounds of beans, to be divided equally among 7 families. How much does each family get?

52. Tina has 8 friends, and she spends 9 minutes per friend sending a message. How many minutes does she spend sending messages?

53. 28 cards are dealt out equally to 4 people. How many cards does each person get?

54. 4 vans carry 6 people each. How many people do the vans carry in all?

55. Each of 5 people owns 2 pairs of shoes. How many pairs of shoes do they own in all?

56. A recipe uses 4 ounces of ketchup. Someone wants to make 3 times as much as the recipe makes. How many ounces of ketchup should be in the new recipe?

57. There are 9 members of a club. Each pays dues of 7 dollars apiece. How much in all does the club collect in dues?

Which op

58. A club wants to collect 72 dollars in dues. There are 9 members. How much should each member be charged?

59. Someone wants to write an 81 page story. The person can write 9 pages each day. How many days will it take for the person to write the story?

60. I have 14 bags of grapes that I want to give out equally among my two children. How much does each child get?

61. I have 35 minutes left to talk to customers, and 7 of them are in line. If I want to give each of them the same amount of time, how much time can I spend with each?

62. Cynthia wants to practice her dance routine 10 times tonight. She has practiced it 7 times. How many more does she have to go?

A only

63. Cynthia practices her dance 10 times each night. How many times does she practice it in 9 days?

64. 48 cards are dealt out evenly to some people; each person got 8 cards. How many people were there?

65. 49 cards are dealt out evenly to 7 people. How many cards does each person get?

66. I want to go 21 miles; I can travel 7 miles per hour. How long will the trip take me?

67. I go 36 miles in 4 hours. How many miles per hour do I go, on the average?

68. It takes 2 lemons for Sam to make a liter of lemonade. How many lemons will it take to make 5 liters of lemonade?

69. A dog is supposed to get 2 milligrams of medicine for every kilogram of the dog's mass. If the dog weighs 8 kilograms, how many milligrams of medicine should the dog get?

70. If each person makes an average of 5 doctor visits a year, how many total doctor visits were made by 7 people in the year?

71. There are 15 kids in a group. They get into groups of 3 for an activity. How many groups do they form?

72. Molly spends 30 dollars for each of her textbooks. If she buys five textbooks, how much does she spend total?

73. Sven gets 9 dollars an hour. How long does he have to work to earn 72 dollars?

74. Someone runs 5 meters per second for 10 seconds. How many meters does the person go?

75. Each person in a family has 3 suitcases. They have 18 suitcases in all. How many people are in the family?

Word Problems Involving All 4 Operations

Which op

76. A plant grows 5 inches each month. How much does it grow in 6 months?

77. In a bunch of ducks, with two legs each, there are a total of 18 legs. How many ducks are there?

78. Alice's car goes 30 miles per gallon of gas. How far does the car go on 10 gallons?

79. John can type 100 characters per minute. How long will it take him to type 500 characters?

80. Linda gets paid 3 dollars for each page she types. How many pages does she have to type to earn 21 dollars?

81. Linda gets paid 3 dollars for each page she types. How much does she earn from typing 5 pages?

82. Each glass of orange juice has 100 calories. How many calories are in 5 glasses of orange juice?

83. Jack has 3 flash drives. Each holds 2 gigabytes of information. How many gigabytes can his drives hold altogether?

A only

84. Rashad wants to store 12 gigabytes of information on flash drives, each of which holds 4 gigabytes. How many flash drives does Rashad need?

85. Tom wants to copy 15 gigabytes of information. He has already copied 7 gigabytes. How many does he have left to copy?

86. Julie has two flash drives, one holding 8 gigabytes and another holding 4 gigabytes. How much information can the two flash drives hold in all?

87. A person has 20 files in his file cabinet. Each one weighs two newtons. How many newtons do the 20 files weigh altogether?

88. A nut has a mass of 5 grams. How many nuts does it take to have a mass of 30 grams?

89. A cup is 8 ounces. How many cups does it take to make 64 ounces?

90. There are two pints in a quart. How many pints are in 8 quarts?

Which op

91. A computer battery will stay charged for 3 hours. If the person wants to use the computer for 15 hours, how many times must the battery be charged (counting the first charge before the computer is used)?

92. Someone makes a flag with 5 rows of stars, and 4 stars in each row (that is, 4 columns). How many stars are there altogether?

93. 30 people are going somewhere, and 5 people can fit in each car. How many cars are needed to take the 30 people?

94. It's 6 miles from town A to town B, and then 5 more miles from town B to town C. If someone goes from A to B to C, how far have they gone?

95. If someone walks 10 meters north, and then comes back 3 meters south, how far is the person from the starting point?

96. It takes someone 10 minutes to type a page. How long does it take to type 3 pages?

97. Someone takes a total of 15 milligrams of a chemical, and puts an equal amount into each of three beakers. How much goes into each beaker?

98. A phone weighs 2 newtons. A second phone weighs 10 newtons. The second phone weighs how many times as much as the first?

99. A phone weighs 3 newtons. A second phone weighs 3 times as much. How much does the second phone weigh?

100. A book weighs 12 newtons. It weighs 4 times as much as a smaller book. How much does the smaller book weigh?

Practicing Task-Switching with Reading Words

If there's a skill that's even more important for school success than math facts, it's the ability to read. Most students will benefit from lots of practice in reading individual words. The skill of "phonemic awareness" is that of hearing the individual sounds in words, and blending those sounds together. This is a very important skill for fluent reading. To develop this skill, as well as to practice recognizing lots of words, it's good to do "sounding and blending": this means, for example, upon seeing the word "fit," saying, "fuh ih tuh fit." Seeing a word and saying the "sounds only," for example seeing the word "get" and saying "guh eh tuh," also give practice in phonemic awareness. It's also good reading practice, of course, just to look at a word and just read it, or to "blend only." If the word is in a numbered list, you can do "blend only" with and without saying the item number first.

So we have four conditions: "S and B" (sound and blend), "S only" (sounds only), "B only" (blend only), and "Num and B" (number and blend). We can do task-switching among those four ways of responding to numbered words, while we're at the same time getting in lots of good reading practice.

The words in the lists that follow start with short vowel consonant-vowel-consonant words, and gradually go up the hierarchy of reading difficulty. These lists follow the same general order as those in my book, *Manual for Tutors and Teachers of Reading*. In the reading manual, the jumps in difficulty from one list to the next are much smaller. There is much more attention to the prerequisite skills worth shoring up before taking on word lists. But for some students, the words in this task-switching manual may be enough, especially combined with what the student learns at school. The best of all possible worlds may be to use the reading manual and to use task-switching with these lists as a supplementary activity and review.

I recommend ignoring the directions and practicing the lists with one set of directions only – especially sounding and blending – before taking on the task-switching.

As with all of these lists, the real reward comes from doing them repeatedly and setting new speed records as time goes by.

Three Phoneme Short Vowel Words

For "B only," (that is, "Blend only") when you see bug, say "bug." For "S and B," (or "Sound and Blend") when you see bug, say "buh uh guh, bug."

S and B
1. fuss
2. top
3. tap
4. mat
5. pat
6. pet
7. log
8. nap
B only
9. keg
10. pop
11. jazz
12. kiss
13. get
14. not
15. den
16. run
17. sum
18. ham
19. Nat
20. pad
S and B
21. fit
22. men
23. kill
24. mud
25. nip
26. bed
27. miss
28. Gus
29. rap
30. Jill
31. tax

32. bin
33. hut
B only
34. puff
35. cuff
36. bat
37. moss
38. pan
39. tug
40. nut
41. fed
42. wag
43. tell
S and B
44. hag
45. Kim
46. sin
47. less
48. set
49. lid
50. bag
51. hug
S and B
52. Tom
53. kit
54. rib
B only
55. tip
56. rod
57. fog
58. fill
59. led
60. fell
61. mug

62. gull
63. rip
64. cob
65. web
66. pod
67. gun
68. dot
69. wax
S and B
70. tub
71. tag
72. tiff
73. toss
74. mum
75. nod
76. jam
B only
77. hot
78. Ben
79. Tim
80. buzz
81. bill
82. lip
83. sis
84. fan
S and B
85. fig
86. Jim
87. hen
88. hiss
89. bit
90. dad
91. tan
92. Don

93. hum
94. vet
95. nun
B only
96. sell
97. net
98. job
99. rub
100. red

Short Vowel Words

For "S only," (that is, "Sound only") when you see bug, say "buh uh guh."

S only
1. splint
2. next
3. bag
4. drill
5. land
6. pest
7. let
8. stamp
9. lid
10. dogs
11. rip
B only
12. gulp
13. swell
14. strip
15. set
16. cuff
17. God
18. dim
19. grip
S only
20. slink
21. boss
22. crack
23. lips
24. had
25. ink
26. jam
B only
27. will
28. pigs
29. nun
30. tell
31. span

32. fund
33. swim
34. rock
35. belt
36. job
37. brim
S only
38. help
39. fuzz
40. swept
41. if
42. tug
43. desk
44. bond
45. dusk
46. mass
47. wigs
S only
48. wag
49. pan
50. damp
B only
51. clamp
52. prompt
53. kill
54. pass
55. mutt
S only
56. trip
57. moss
58. mats
59. beg
60. drip
61. ham
62. ax

63. well
64. an
65. nut
66. bump
B only
67. sell
68. spend
69. toss
70. did
71. up
72. lift
73. drink
74. puff
75. till
76. pod
77. hops
78. luck
79. guns
80. lick
81. hum
S only
82. bring
83. from
84. pant
85. hill
86. lock
87. Fran
88. fond
89. dunk
B only
90. mix
91. wish
92. skip
93. silk
94. strong

95. pack
96. pin
97. tank
98. stem
99. lip
100. pub

Short Vowel Words, with sh, th, ch, wh, and qu

For "Num and B" (that is, "Number and Blend") when you see 1. bug, say "One, bug."

Num and B	32. tag	64. black	96. snap
1. shot	33. sketch	65. link	97. snatch
2. sing	34. nap	S and B	98. run
3. odd	35. slip	66. stuff	99. bet
4. peg	36. bunch	67. back	Num and B
5. shift	37. glint	68. mush	100. moth
6. tan	Num and B	69. brink	
7. hop	38. slack	70. pond	
8. with	39. when	71. sells	
9. dress	40. hog	72. plump	
10. tax	41. rap	73. max	
S and B	42. cuts	74. gun	
11. rips	43. bulk	Num and B	
12. send	44. fan	75. fill	
13. must	45. whack	76. mad	
14. drug	S and B	77. log	
15. fed	46. shut	78. ship	
16. wing	47. rust	79. trap	
17. sob	48. trick	80. web	
18. notch	49. chick	81. wind	
Num and B	50. fact	82. past	
19. cloth	51. him	83. fist	
20. glad	52. wax	84. left	
21. bus	53. hunch	85. Don	
22. trot	54. flip	S and B	
23. cash	Num and B	86. whip	
24. kick	55. crib	87. sis	
25. chop	56. tuck	88. cob	
26. brisk	57. huff	89. cuffs	
27. pick	58. brag	90. mud	
S and B	59. than	91. last	
28. lung	60. quilt	92. bit	
29. tap	61. rim	93. mum	
30. brat	62. fix	94. risk	
31. sad	63. then	95. stuck	

More Short Vowel Words

B only
1. fetch
2. yank
3. frog
4. bench
5. hum
6. nip
7. flock
8. mug
9. brand
10. sack
11. spell
S and B
12. bluff
13. leg
14. less
15. frank
16. hums
17. six
18. tent
19. this
20. stub
21. Nick
B only
22. hen
23. cats
24. bed
25. Ken
26. junk
27. cot
S and B
28. quick
29. went
30. bath
31. much
32. Fred

33. lot
34. hills
35. string
36. Tim
B only
37. ox
38. click
39. splash
40. jazz
41. beds
42. gull
43. batch
S and B
44. stretch
45. mock
46. ditch
47. mist
48. chum
49. kid
50. hats
51. led
52. such
53. quill
B only
54. gift
55. that
56. nest
57. slot
58. digs
59. flop
60. hug
61. sock
62. bugs
S and B
63. zip
64. thrift

65. den
66. snip
67. sips
68. patch
69. plank
70. tin
B only
71. pinch
72. pad
73. king
74. rank
75. brush
76. mask
77. pen
78. pump
79. dell
80. rib
S and B
81. muff
82. plum
83. shop
84. melt
85. hit
86. bets
87. elf
88. held
89. lamp
90. rash
B only
91. mess
92. strap
93. dock
94. lap
95. drum
96. gash
S and B

97. dust
98. print
99. its
100. bang

Long Vowel Words, Set 1

B only
1. hold
2. own
3. dry
4. cone
5. street
6. Zeke
7. tail
8. go

S only
9. steam
10. fade
11. dole
12. boat
13. slay

B only
14. flies
15. note
16. maze
17. steer
18. froze
19. taste
20. blaze

S only
21. shine
22. low
23. mine
24. grind
25. hire
26. load
27. Mike
28. cheat
29. seed
30. throne
31. chore
32. sight

33. sale
34. wife
35. stream

B only
36. size
37. made
38. ago
39. heat
40. chime
41. stripe
42. hello
43. woe
44. chain
45. reach
46. dine
47. rate
48. make

S only
49. boast
50. seal
51. tape
52. lean
53. hate
54. green
55. faint
56. mow
57. plain
58. goal
59. shy
60. grope

B only
61. brave
62. height
63. thigh
64. toad
65. fright

66. leap
67. breed
68. male
69. fume
70. doe
71. knight

S only
72. five
73. whine
74. blame
75. spray
76. hue
77. deep
78. sail
79. gripe

B only
80. throw
81. pie
82. cry
83. old
84. pine
85. frail
86. dear
87. cheap
88. tight
89. Poe
90. hive

S only
91. sleep
92. weep
93. pure
94. oak
95. peak
96. wheat
97. hail
98. spade

99. pail
100. he

Long Vowel Words, Set 2

S and B
1. meet
2. goat
3. queer
4. tube
5. most
6. may
7. Luke
8. moan
9. snail
10. oath
11. maid
Num and B
12. hear
13. toll
14. bind
15. peep
16. waste
17. teeth
18. blow
19. ripe
20. claim
21. flow
S and B
22. peach
23. die
24. reap
25. screen
26. train
27. lame
28. shore
29. nine
30. life
31. feel
32. wait
Num and B

33. throat
34. way
35. wore
36. colt
37. roe
38. ear
39. robe
40. try
S and B
41. slope
42. fight
43. growth
44. spite
45. tame
46. ape
47. fate
48. light
49. feet
50. game
51. like
52. creep
53. maybe
Num and B
54. safe
55. pry
56. flake
57. joke
58. aid
59. rake
60. ride
61. fry
62. pain
63. braid
64. blind
65. bright
S and B

66. seen
67. bray
68. cure
69. steel
70. plate
71. crime
72. saint
Num and B
73. bite
74. glide
75. tea
76. coast
77. while
78. foam
79. poll
80. bee
81. more
82. eve
83. rope
84. wire
85. east
86. lute
87. rind
S and B
88. use
89. clear
90. date
91. faith
92. haze
93. teach
94. bean
95. side
Num and B
96. ray
97. dome
98. toe

99. brute
100. sheer

Long Vowel Words, Set 3

S and B
1. beak
2. away
3. moat
4. near
5. hoe
6. trade
7. clay
8. rule
9. tire
10. might
11. quaint
12. spoke
13. fly

B only
14. grain
15. by
16. loaf
17. peel
18. zeal
19. bait
20. vain
21. prune
22. loan
23. leaf

S and B
24. sweep
25. window
26. smoke
27. beach
28. bike
29. eke
30. store

B only
31. paint
32. speech

33. crate
34. spy
35. foe
36. rail
37. Crete
38. home
39. aim
40. glow
41. fire
42. dream

S and B
43. night
44. lay
45. wake
46. yeast
47. cope
48. tried
49. cream
50. strain
51. dive
52. grate
53. bay

B only
54. bolt
55. bore
56. see
57. cane
58. heel
59. yellow
60. lobe
61. before

S and B
62. Joe
63. brain
64. Dave
65. globe

66. pane
67. jay
68. scroll
69. cube
70. smile
71. don't
72. woke

B only
73. tune
74. Pete
75. wide
76. roast
77. soap
78. told
79. shave
80. she
81. gear
82. flea
83. cold
84. play
85. fake
86. dune
87. shape

S and B
88. flute
89. bride
90. stole
91. groan
92. child
93. fear
94. wild
95. fried

B only
96. tone
97. heap
98. fine

99. quake
100. meat

94

Words With Vowel Blends, Set 1

B only
1. corn
2. pall
3. food
4. Sue
5. shook
S only
6. girl
7. under
8. stern
9. arch
10. talk
11. grouch
12. marsh
13. claw
B only
14. woo
15. dew
16. hurl
17. bound
18. south
19. torch
20. glue
21. cook
22. moo
23. smooth
24. scar
25. star
26. form
27. part
28. gown
S only
29. flour
30. vowel
31. loop
32. tall

33. too
34. always
35. about
B only
36. cloud
37. art
38. malt
39. dirt
40. chalk
41. stall
42. porch
43. round
44. gaunt
45. never
46. farm
47. lord
S only
48. cord
49. point
50. hound
51. fool
52. burr
53. soon
54. sharp
55. bark
56. howl
57. vow
58. chart
59. shirt
60. mouth
B only
61. yarn
62. scout
63. ever
64. tool
65. sprawl

66. halt
67. drown
68. straw
S only
69. booth
70. burn
71. cool
72. jerk
73. stew
74. powder
75. hoist
76. dark
77. pouch
78. draw
79. worn
B only
80. fowl
81. found
82. law
83. Carl
84. hard
85. far
86. tooth
87. boot
88. port
89. third
S only
90. foot
91. proud
92. flaunt
93. spout
94. dart
95. twirl
96. birch
97. hers
S only

98. shark
99. crown
100. brow

Vowel Blends, Set 2

Num and B
1. news
2. coy
3. crew
4. haunt
5. true
6. drool
7. haul
8. jaunt
9. skirt
10. balk

S and B
11. room
12. surf
13. saw
14. brown
15. car
16. short
17. curb
18. drawn
19. thirst
20. hook
21. mood

Num and B
22. fault
23. our
24. shoot
25. card
26. or
27. birth
28. purr
29. fall

S and B
30. scoop
31. starch
32. jar

33. soy
34. toy
35. north
36. firm
37. church
38. sort
39. good
40. pool

Num and B
41. root
42. how
43. snort
44. cork
45. new
46. daunt
47. horn
48. doom
49. stoop
50. taunt
51. mall
52. thorn

S and B
53. pork
54. crawl
55. thaw
56. fork
57. couch
58. ground
59. flew
60. bird
61. hood
62. moon
63. zoo
64. scorch
65. frown

Num and B

66. trout
67. bow
68. spoil
69. gall
70. squall
71. soot
72. fir
73. hoop
74. launch
75. broil
76. paw
77. stool
78. salt
79. march
80. sworn

S and B
81. shawl
82. shout
83. lard
84. sport
85. bawl
86. for
87. paunch

Num and B
88. spoon
89. bald
90. brew
91. strewn
92. coin

S and B
93. hoof
94. lark
95. loin
96. pound
97. foil
98. flaw

99. brood
100. house

Vowel Blends, Set 3

B only
1. raw
2. Roy
3. dawn
4. jaw
5. clue
6. wall
7. gloom
8. blew
9. Paul
10. whirl
11. scorn
S and B
12. start
13. ball
14. cow
15. broom
16. ouch
17. now
18. call
19. joy
20. all
21. tar
22. owl
23. stir
B only
24. roof
25. burst
26. fraud
27. book
28. around
29. troop
30. crouch
31. harm
32. joint
33. stalk

34. sir
S and B
35. scarf
36. perch
37. darn
38. coo
39. torn
40. due
41. squirm
42. soil
43. out
44. down
B only
45. walk
46. loud
47. herd
48. bloom
49. storm
50. pout
51. stood
S and B
52. arm
53. ploy
54. moist
55. after
56. wood
57. took
58. clown
59. mark
60. Bert
61. wow
62. yawn
63. wool
64. small
65. foul
66. Jew

B only
67. first
68. her
69. look
70. hall
71. grew
72. sour
73. spool
74. sound
75. drew
76. oil
77. town
78. turn
79. furl
S and B
80. yard
81. haunch
82. snout
83. groom
84. growl
B only
85. smart
86. spur
87. chew
88. boy
89. park
90. strew
91. hurt
92. chirp
S and B
93. lawn
94. blue
95. droop
96. clerk
97. Walt
98. bar

99. cart
100. lurch

Words With Other Letter-Sound Correspondences, Set 1

B only
1. asked
2. sonny
3. since
4. gnome
5. bought
6. matched
7. knelt
8. treads
S only
9. ledge
10. daughter
11. money
12. baked
13. forced
14. gem
15. tipped
16. comb
17. noise
18. son
19. mare
B only
20. closed
21. earth
22. forge
23. parked
24. loathe
25. place
26. swamp
27. hushed
28. ounce
29. sniffed
30. germ
31. rolled
S only
32. easy

33. fiend
34. wealth
35. pear
36. trailed
37. naught
38. heads
39. glove
40. enough
41. breathe
42. mice
43. dumb
44. those
B only
45. heaven
46. flare
47. hissed
48. push
49. spaced
50. break
51. bull
52. orange
53. field
54. feather
55. slice
56. cracked
57. wreath
58. cause
59. fished
S only
60. smudge
61. fierce
62. mixed
63. kneel
64. race
65. sailed
66. bulge

67. helped
B only
68. yield
69. puffed
70. glare
71. robbed
72. breath
73. seethe
74. rise
75. ton
76. wretch
77. taught
S only
78. sledge
79. scratched
80. knock
81. wrist
82. tough
83. weight
84. sludge
85. is
86. pearl
87. want
88. canned
B only
89. cough
90. month
91. swan
92. fuse
93. snapped
94. change
95. threat
S only
96. siege
97. George
98. glanced

99. pounce
100. hose

98

Words With Other Letter-Sound Correspondences, Set 2

Num and B
1. jerked
2. wise
3. hair
4. eighty
5. strange
6. cent
7. rouse
8. instead
9. death
10. chair
11. written
S and B
12. brief
13. wiped
14. cell
15. dread
16. splashed
17. lair
18. gym
19. priest
20. caught
21. brought
22. pledge
23. thieves
24. cage
25. lace
26. dead
Num and B
27. called
28. trapped
29. skipped
30. dodge
31. heard
32. bridge
33. spread

34. edge
S and B
35. pause
36. kissed
37. ace
38. heavy
39. honey
40. raced
41. budge
42. love
43. knob
44. these
45. shriek
46. soothe
Num and B
47. squeezed
48. as
49. laugh
50. share
51. balked
52. please
53. flair
54. blare
55. limb
56. raise
57. growled
S and B
58. crashed
59. patched
60. above
61. steady
62. rough
Num and B
63. excuse
64. air
65. sleigh

66. gnaw
67. use
68. urge
69. ought
70. helped
71. wrong
72. wage
73. wheeled
74. health
75. brace
S and B
76. eight
77. rare
78. meant
79. pinched
80. thumb
81. breakfast
82. preached
83. chance
84. smoked
85. lodge
Num and B
86. Butch
87. stitched
88. choice
89. gnu
90. wrestle
91. front
92. great
S and B
93. sweater
94. monkey
95. crawled
96. monks
97. niece
98. those

99. shrieked
100. page

Words With Other Letter-Sound Correspondences, Set 3

B only
1. nagged
2. pierce
3. wished
4. stair
5. because
6. freight
7. filled
8. square
9. pull
10. wall
11. bear
12. pair
S and B
13. huffed
14. tease
15. hare
16. thread
17. knife
18. wretched
19. bush
20. whipped
21. pace
22. hedge
23. snare
B only
24. nose
25. close
26. sweat
27. peace
28. pinned
S and B
29. bathe
30. knee
31. dropped
32. thought

33. fought
34. learn
35. watch
36. steak
37. chief
38. wrote
39. charmed
40. deaf
41. fringe
B only
42. neighbor
43. bread
44. search
45. sneezed
46. fixed
47. weigh
48. answer
49. crumb
50. naughty
51. write
S and B
52. prince
53. jumped
54. fudge
55. nudge
56. fare
57. wrap
58. ready
B only
59. cinch
60. cheese
61. wash
62. gnat
63. huge
64. know
65. twice

66. put
67. stopped
68. voice
69. scare
70. hitched
71. stare
72. fair
73. stage
S and B
74. spare
75. leather
76. care
77. spruce
78. choose
79. shield
80. age
81. gene
82. dance
83. debt
84. slammed
B only
85. wreck
86. sought
87. wear
88. Bruce
89. face
90. known
91. water
92. aware
S and B
93. stacked
94. leaped
95. tripped
96. wan
97. daisy
98. rage

99. played
100. whole

Polysyllabic Words, Set 1

S only
1. wor ry   worry
2. tip ping   tipping
3. fit ting   fitting
4. bath tub   bathtub
5. rid dle   riddle
6. hur ries   hurries
7. drum mer   drummer
8. wel come   welcome
9. some one   someone
10. butch er   butcher
11. com pan ies   companies
12. him self himself
13. anx ious   anxious
14. can ning   canning
15. class room   classroom

B only
16. set tle   settle
17. brit tle   brittle
18. Pe ter   Peter
19. be came   became
20. nut ty   nutty
21. sin gle   single
22. car ries   carries
23. in flu ence   influence
24. ca per   caper
25. frac tion   fraction
26. big ger   bigger

S only
27. wai ter   waiter
28. fun ny   funny
29. pos si ble   possible
30. mo ment   moment
31. ver y   very
32. pat ted   patted
33. pre tend   pretend

34. act ed   acted

B only
35. fair ies   fairies
36. on ly   only
37. hug ging   hugging
38. con fi dence   confidence
39. nag ging   nagging
40. co zy   cozy
41. birth day   birthday

S only
42. home work   homework
43. un cle   uncle
44. lath er   lather
45. Mon day   Monday
46. la cy   lacy
47. real ly   really
48. jeal ous   jealous
49. gra vy   gravy
50. driz zle   drizzle
51. dan ces   dances

B only
52. ba bies   babies
53. joy ous   joyous
54. or ange   orange
55. jost le   jostle
56. pur ring   purring
57. fer ment   ferment
58. fu ture   future
59. men tion   mention
60. sum mer   summer
61. like ly   likely
62. bod ies   bodies

S only
63. rail road   railroad
64. tum bler   tumbler
65. co ping   coping

66. la zy   lazy
67. trim ming   trimming
B only
68. aw ful   awful
69. trea sure   treasure
70. o bey   obey
71. fair y   fairy
72. book case   bookcase
73. flick er   flicker
74. cau tious   cautious
75. la dy   lady
76. ti tle   title
77. point ed   pointed
78. ship ping   shipping
79. grum ble   grumble
80. gar den   garden
S only
81. six teen   sixteen
82. e nor mous   enormous
83. plat ter   platter
84. ho ping   hoping
85. act or   actor
86. mail box   mailbox
87. dig it   digit
88. hob ble   hobble
89. plea sant   pleasant
90. sil li est   silliest
91. fa ces   faces
92. dan gle   dangle
B only
93. re quire ment   requirement
94. belt way   beltway
95. ba by   baby
96. oft en   often
97. broth er   brother
B only
98. el ev a tor   elevator
99. ci der   cider
100. en er gy   energy

Polysyllabic Words, Set 2

S and B
1. rath er   rather
2. hop ping   hopping
3. nee dle   needle
4. ug li er   uglier
5. com pli ance   compliance
6. sa ving   saving
7. in side   inside
8. cour age   courage

Num and B
9. gen er al   general
10. fla vor   flavor
11. pep per   pepper
12. count ed   counted
13. ad mit   admit
14. wrest le   wrestle
15. sad ly   sadly
16. son ny   sonny
17. mix ture   mixture
18. hap pi est   happiest
19. ex pect   expect
20. mer cy   mercy

S and B
21. ad vice   advice
22. grand mom   grandmom
23. ex cite ment   excitement
24. some how   somehow
25. wea ver   weaver
26. tri umph   triumph
27. dam age   damage
28. jun gle   jungle
29. sai lor   sailor
30. rust le   rustle
31. let ting   letting
32. un til   until
33. ber ries   berries

Num and B
34. gath er   gather
35. pro duc tive   productive
36. tack le   tackle
37. din ner   dinner
38. dip per   dipper
39. tur tle   turtle
40. hap pi er   happier
41. la ter   later
42. some bod y   somebody
43. ques tion   question
44. friend ship   friendship
45. po nies   ponies
46. won der   wonder
47. fam i ly   family
48. cow ard   coward

S and B
49. a bove   above
50. cud dle   cuddle
51. crack le   crackle
52. a wake   awake
53. lick ing   licking
54. cu ri ous   curious
55. jug gler   juggler
56. sus pi cious   suspicious
57. Sun day   Sunday
58. ev er y   every
59. pump kin   pumpkin

Num and B
60. up per   upper
61. im por tance   importance
62. min cing   mincing
63. dig ging   digging
64. rub ber   rubber
65. chil ly   chilly
66. na ming   naming

67. ap pear ance   appearance
S and B
68. na tive   native
69. cig ar   cigar
70. cab bage   cabbage
71. with er   wither
72. en gin eer   engineer
73. tow er   tower
74. fum ble   fumble
Num and B
75. res i dence   residence
76. rug ged   rugged
77. el e phant   elephant
78. cha fing   chafing
79. ex plain   explain
S and B
80. com fort   comfort
81. snap py   snappy
82. watch dog   watchdog
83. fath er   father
84. oun ces   ounces
85. sad dle   saddle
86. an i mal   animal
87. for ti tude   fortitude
88. u ni ted   united
89. sled ding   sledding
90. puz zle   puzzle
Num and B
91. trou ble   trouble
92. ce ment   cement
93. ra ting   rating
94. skim ming   skimming
95. dan ger   danger
96. ad di tion   addition
97. Phil ip   Philip
98. Peg gy   Peggy
99. move ment   movement
100. fib bing   fibbing

Polysyllabic Words, Set 3

B only
1. oth er   other
2. ap ple   apple
3. cush ion   cushion
4. a mount   amount
5. near ly   nearly
6. stor y   story
7. moth er   mother
8. tor ture   torture
9. ex am ple   example
10. tug boat   tugboat

S and B
11. hap py   happy
12. gar bage   garbage
13. jin gle   jingle
14. na vy   navy
15. po ny   pony
16. fic tion   fiction
17. fa ding   fading
18. be come   become
19. hon ey   honey
20. vo ter   voter
21. vi sion   vision

B only
22. dur ing   during
23. fa vor   favor
24. hard ly   hardly
25. trai tor   traitor
26. phras ing   phrasing
27. vis i tor   visitor
28. sun set   sunset
29. na tur al   natural
30. gra ting   grating
31. pen sion   pension
32. at ten tive   attentive
33. snug gle   snuggle

S and B
34. pam phlet   pamphlet
35. man gle   mangle
36. can dy   candy
37. scur ried   scurried
38. be lief   belief
39. quit ting   quitting
40. sick le   sickle
41. ket tle   kettle

B only
42. pas sive   passive
43. brown ie   brownie
44. spe cial   special
45. kit ty   kitty
46. act ive   active
47. skip ping   skipping
48. com pare   compare
49. fan cy   fancy
50. guz zle   guzzle
51. la ser   laser
52. han dy   handy
53. or der   order
54. vis it   visit
55. brim ming   brimming
56. cin der   cinder

S and B
57. par ty   party
58. tan gle   tangle
59. coun try   country
60. log jam   logjam
61. stin gy   stingy
62. tug ging   tugging
63. win ner   winner
64. per mis sion   permission
65. per form ance   performance
66. cou ple   couple

67. slip ping   slipping

B only

68. set ting   setting

69. stud y   study

70. care ful   careful

71. gro cer ies   groceries

72. gin ger   ginger

S and B

73. tro phy   trophy

74. pho net ic   phonetic

75. hast en   hasten

76. de cide   decide

77. de li cious   delicious

78. re joice   rejoice

79. bla ming   blaming

80. vi cious   vicious

81. in come   income

82. en gine   engine

83. hyph en   hyphen

84. pad ded   padded

85. truth ful   truthful

B only

86. bless ed   blessed

87. thir ty   thirty

88. siz zle   sizzle

89. col lect   collect

90. lei sure   leisure

91. be gan   began

92. mat ted   matted

93. slo ping   sloping

S and B

94. Bob by   Bobby

95. pen cil   pencil

96. cen ter   center

97. cap tive   captive

98. foot ball   football

99. au tumn   autumn

100. play ground   playground

Polysyllabic Words, Set 4

S and B
1. man u al   manual
2. ac tiv i ty   activity
3. sit u a tion   situation
4. di rec tions   directions
5. stim u lus   stimulus
6. var i a tion   variation
7. dif fi cult   difficult
8. con cen tra tion   concentration
9. pos si ble   possible
10. sep ar ate ly   separately
11. prac tic ing   practicing
B only
12. pho ne mic   phonemic
13. a ware ness   awareness
14. med i cine   medicine
15. im prove   improve
16. stim u late   stimulate
17. im pulse   impulse
18. de ci sion   decision
19. pos sib il i ty   possibility
20. i mag ine   imagine
21. in for ma tion   information
22. mem o ry   memory
23. re mem ber ing   remembering
24. sup posed   supposed
25. cor rect ly   correctly
26. fre quent ly   frequently
S and B
27. par tic u lar ly   particularly
28. def ic it   deficit
29. sim i lar   similar
30. chal lenged   challenged
31. dis or der   disorder
32. var i ous   various
33. e lec tron ic   electronic

34. de pend ing   depending
B only
35. tempt a tion   temptation
36. vid e o games   videogames
37. strat e gy   strategy
38. re act ing   reacting
39. ex act ly   exactly
40. ne ces sar y   necessary
41. care ful ly   carefully
42. com pu ter   computer
43. def in ite ly   definitely
44. mar ried   married
45. dras tic al ly   drastically
46. ex am ple   example
S and B
47. fire fight er   firefighter
48. o ver come   overcome
49. real is tic   realistic
50. cau tious   cautious
51. sec tion   section
52. in volved   involved
53. re spond ed   responded
54. im por tant   important
55. a bil i ty   ability
56. prob ab ly   probably
57. gen er al ize   generalize
B only
58. ev i dence   evidence
59. pre front al   prefrontal
60. cor tex   cortex
61. strength ened   strengthened
62. in tense   intense
S and B
63. ment al   mental
64. re search   research
65. ad vanced   advanced

66. en ter tain ing   entertaining
67. com pet ent   competent
68. fol low ing   following
69. el e ment ar y   elementary
70. di rec tions   directions
71. phys i cal   physical
72. re spond   respond
73. di vi ded   divided
74. prod uct   product
75. ab brev i ate   abbreviate
B only
76. switch ing   switching
77. syl la ble   syllable
78. sec tion   section
79. op er a tion   operation
80. au to mat i cal ly   automatically
81. ca reer   career
82. ea si er   easier
83. cal cu la tor   calculator
S and B
84. rea son a ble   reasonable
85. pro nounce   pronounce
86. flu ent ly   fluently
87. hi er arch y   hierarchy
88. ar rang ing   arranging
89. frus tra ted   frustrated
90. dis cip line   discipline
B only
91. for tu nate ly   fortunately
92. rap id ly   rapidly
93. com fort ab ly   comfortably
94. tre men dous   tremendous
95. real ize   realize
96. pro fi cient   proficient
97. pro ce dure   procedure
98. ad di tion al   additional
99. av er age   average
100. es tim ate   estimate

The Scientific Literature on Task-Switching

Do people with ADHD have trouble with task-switching?

Cepeda et al. (2000) calculated "switch costs" in the same way that we have described in this book. They found that "ADHD children showed substantially larger switch costs than non-ADHD children." (page 213)

King et al. (2007) compared adults with ADHD to adults without ADHD on two task-switching activities. These authors conclude: "Evidence for ADHD group impaired interference control was obtained from both tasks. Task switching group error rate profiles revealed distinct cognitive flexibility deficiencies in the ADHD group." (page 12)

Boonstra et al. (2010) studied forty-nine adults with ADHD compared with forty-nine normal control adults, matched for age and gender. The participants were given a large battery of tests, including those that, like task-switching, are thought to be measure of executive functioning as well as other intellectual tasks not thought to involve executive functioning. "After stringent controls for nonexecutive function demands and IQ, adults with ADHD

showed problems in inhibition and set shifting but not in any of the other executive functioning domains tested." (page 209)

Rhodes et al. (2005) found that a group of children with ADHD showed impairment on an "attentional set-shifting" task on the Cambridge Neuropsychological Test Automated Battery (CANTAB). However, the authors of this study also found deficits in the ADHD sample in other intellectual tasks, such as paired associates learning. Thus this study does not support the specificity of task-switching impairment in ADHD.

In another negative study, Sheres et al. (2004) compared boys with ADHD with normal control boys on various tests of executive functioning, as well as other intellectual tasks. The boys with ADHD demonstrated deficits in "interference control [and] inhibition of an ongoing response," however, after controlling for age, IQ, and non-executive functioning measures, none of the executive functioning deficits remained significant.

Gualtieri and Johnson (2008) found that on a computerized screening battery including a task-switching test, "significant differences were detected between normals and untreated ADHD patients." (p 459)

Goth-Owens et al. (2010) report slower performances of children with ADHD inattentive type on a set-shifting task than those of controls.

Is task-switching related to higher achievement and greater mental development?

St Clair-Thompson and Gathercole (2006) found that children with better "updating abilities" had better working memory, and those with better working memory in turn had higher achievement in English and mathematics.

Davidson et al. (2006) studied the development of task-switching as children grew older from age 4 to age 13 and in young adults. Children in this age range showed better performance as they got older; 13 year-olds were still not at adult levels on task-switching. "Effects seen only in reaction time in adults were seen primarily in accuracy in young children. Adults slowed down on difficult trials to preserve accuracy; but the youngest children were impulsive; their reaction times remained more constant but at an accuracy cost on difficult trials." (p 2037) Luciana and Nelson (1998) also found a "general age-related progression in ability levels" on "frontal lobe tasks," of which task-switching is one. Four-year-

olds performed worse than 5- to 7-year-olds on all measures.

Is the severity of ADHD correlated with the degree of difficulty in task-switching?

Oades and Christiansen (2008) reported that "The latency for completion of the trail-making task controlling for psychomotor processing was longer for ADHD cases, and correlated with Conners' ratings of symptom severity across all subjects." (p. 21)

Are people with ADHD the only group that seems to be at a disadvantage in task-switching?

Meiran et al. (2010) compared patients suffering from unipolar depression, others suffering from obsessive compulsive disorder, and match control participants. Patients with both unipolar depression and obsessive compulsive disorder "required more trials to adjust to single-task conditions after experiencing task-switching."

Kapoula et al. (2010) studied dyslexic teenagers and controls. They found results suggesting "that the inhibitory and attention processes required by the Stroop tests are dysfunctioning even in older dyslexics." Poljac et al. (2010) reported (in a title that well summarizes the article), "Impaired task switching performance in children with dyslexia but not in children with autism."

Wylie et al. (2010) reported that patients with schizophrenia appeared to be more impaired in task-switching than they were in even other executive function tasks.

Roberts et al. (2007) report, using a review and meta-analysis of other studies, that "Problems in set shifting as measured by a variety of neuropsychological tasks are present in people with eating disorders." (p. 1075)

What portion of the brain seems most responsible for task-switching performance?

Rubia et al. (2010) used functional magnetic resonance imaging (fMRI) to look at brain activation during a task-switching activity. "The fMRI comparison showed that the patients with ADHD compared to both control and patients with conduct disorder showed underactivation in right and left inferior prefrontal cortex."

Cubillo et al. (2010) in a study also using fMRI found that "adults with childhood ADHD showed reduced activation compared to controls in bilateral inferior prefrontal cortex, caudate and thalamus... as well as in left parietal lobe during the Switch task."

Robbins (2007) reviewed studies on the neuropsychological basis of task-switching. "Notably, most of the paradigms implicate a locus in the right prefrontal cortex, specifically in the right inferior frontal gyrus."(p 917).

Smith et al. (2006) reported, using functional MRI, that "Boys with ADHD showed decreased activation in .. the bilateral prefrontal and temporal lobes and right parietal lobe during the switch task." (p 957) The boys in this study were medication-naive, thus "suggesting that hypoactivation in this patient group is unrelated to long-term stimulant exposure." (p 957)

Newman et al. (2008) reported that in rats, "Noradrenergic depletion of the medial prefrontal cortex is sufficient to impair attentional set-shifting." (p 39).

Do the medications used for ADHD improve task-switching?

Cepeda et al. (2000), as mentioned above, found that ADHD children showed larger switch costs than non-ADHD children on a task-switching challenge. "However, when on medication, the ADHD children's switch performance was equivalent to control children." (page 213)

Mehta et al. (2004) found that methylphenidate, in a dose of 0.5 mg/kg of body weight, improved "attentional set-shifting" on the CANTAB neuropsychological battery, as well as a couple of other subtests.

Gualtieri and Johnson (2008), using a neuropsychological battery including a task-switching activity, compared medication treated ADHD patients, untreated ADHD patients, and normal subjects. "Treated patients performed better than untreated patients but remained significantly impaired compared to normal subjects." (p 459)

Kramer et al. (2001) asked twenty children with ADHD to perform a task-switching challenge while on and off methylphenidate. "The medication selectively enhanced the children's ability to rapidly and accurately switch between tasks and to focus attention on the currently relevant response set." (page 1277)

However, Rhodes et al. (2006) in a similar study found that, contrary to their predictions, methylphenidate did not enhance performance in a set shifting task.

Can you get better at task-switching by practice?

White and Shah (2006) found that a sample of ADHD adults showed impaired task-switching when compared with non-ADHD adults. Training improved task-switching in both groups.

Berryhill and Hughes (2009) found that a "novel training regimen" reduced task-switching costs to about 20 milliseconds. These investigators also found that the learning of better task switching performance was quite durable: "No decrements in fluent task-switching performance were observed after 10 months without practice."

Buchler et al. (2008) evaluated task-switching performance in young and older adults, and delivered training over 5 days. Training eliminated age effects in task-switching performance.

Newman et al. (2008) found that with rats who had been "noradrenergically lesioned" in the medial prefrontal cortex, "atomoxetine remediated the attentional set-shifting impairments in [lesioned] rats but impaired the [set-shifting] performance of non-lesioned rats. (p. 39). Similarly, Lapiz and Morilak (2006) reported that in rats, "elevating noradrenergic activity at alpha-1 receptors in medial prefrontal cortex facilitates cognitive performance of rats in an attentional set-shifting task, which may contribute to the role of norepinephrine in behavioral state changes such as arousal, or to the beneficial cognitive effects of psychotherapeutic drugs that target noradrenergic neurotransmission." (p. 39)

When you improve at one task-switching challenge, does that generalize to other types of task-switching?

Karbach and Kray (2009) gave training in task-switching to three age groups of participants: ages eight through ten, eighteen through twenty-six, and sixty-two through seventy-six. The investigators reported: "We found near transfer of task-switching training in all age groups, especially in children and older adults. Near transfer was enhanced in adults and impaired in children when training tasks were variable. We also found substantial far transfer to other executive tasks and fluid intelligence in all age groups, pointing to the transfer of relatively general executive control abilities after training." (page 978)

Similarly, the White and Shah (2006) study mentioned above found that training effects of task-switching transferred to other types of task-switching that had not been specifically trained.

Minear and Shah (2008) also report improvement with practice in task-switching, transferable to new situations. These authors state, "These results add to a growing number of studies demonstrating generalizable improvement with training on executive processing." (p 1470)

Does practice on lots of task-switching challenges not only improve task-switching, but also reduce the core symptoms of ADHD?

The core symptoms of ADHD are short attention span (or low work capacity), impulsivity, and hyperactivity. Can one improve these symptoms by enough task-switching practice? This is obviously the most clinically important question, and we have to date not found studies that answer this question.

References

Berryhill, M.E. & Hughes, H.C. (2009). On the minimization of task switch costs following long-term training. *Attention, Perception, and Psychophysics,* 71, 503-514.

Boonstra, A.M., Kooij, J.J., Oosterlaan, J., Sergeant, J.A., & Buitelaar, J.K. (2010). To act or not to act, that's the problem: primarily inhibition difficulties in adult ADHD. *Neuropsychology,* 24, 209-221.

Buchler, N.G., Hoyer, W.J., & Cerella, J. (2008). Rules and more rules: the effects of multiple tasks, extensive training, and aging on task-switching performance. *Memory and Cognition,* 36, 735-748.

Cepeda, N.J., Cepeda, M.L., & Kramer, A.F. (2000). Task switching and attention deficit hyperactivity disorder. *Journal of Abnormal Child Psychology,* 28, 213-226.

Cubillo, A., Halari, R., Ecker, C., Giampietro, V., Taylor, E., & Rubia, K. (2010). Reduced activation and inter-regional functional connectivity of fronto-striatal networks in adults with childhood Attention-Deficit Hyperactivity Disorder (ADHD) and persisting symptoms during tasks of motor inhibition and cognitive switching. *Journal of Psychiatric Research,* Epub ahead of print.

Davidson, M.C., Amso, D., Anderson, L.C., & Diamond, A. (2006). Development of cognitive control and executive functions from 4 to 13 years: evidence from manipulations of memory, inhibition, and task switching. *Neuropsychologia,* 44, 2037-2078.

Goth-Owens, T.L., Martinez-Torteya, C., Martel, M.M., & Nigg, J.T. (2010). Processing Speed Weakness in Children and Adolescents with Non-Hyperactive but Inattentive ADHD (ADD). *Child Neuropsychology.* 16, 1-15.

Gualtieri, C.T. & Johnson, L.G. (2008) Medications do not necessarily normalize cognition in ADHD patients. *Journal of Attention Disorders*, 11, 459-469.

Kapoula, Z., Lê, T.T., Bonnet, A., Bourtoire, P., Demule, E., Fauvel, C., Quilicci, C., & Yang, Q. (2010). Poor Stroop performances in 15-year-old dyslexic teenagers. *Experimental Brain Research,* 203, 419-425.

Karbach, J. & Kray, J. (2009). How useful is executive control training? Age differences in near and far transfer of task-switching training. *Developmental Science,* 12, 978-990.

References

King, J.A., Colla, M., Brass, M., Heuser, I., & von Cramon, D. (2007). Inefficient cognitive control in adult ADHD: evidence from trial-by-trial Stroop test and cued task switching performance. *Behavioral and Brain Functions,* 3, 42.

Kramer, A.F., Cepeda, N.J., & Cepeda, M.L. (2001). Methylphenidate effects on task-switching performance in attention-deficit/hyperactivity disorder. *Journal of the American Academy of Child and Adolescent Psychiatry,* 40, 1277-1284.

Lapiz, M.D. & Morilak, D.A. Noradrenergic modulation of cognitive function in rat medial prefrontal cortex as measured by attentional set shifting capability. *Neuroscience,* 137, 1039-1049.

Luciana, M. & Nelson, C.A. The functional emergence of prefrontally-guided working memory systems in four- to eight-year-old children. *Neuropsychologia,* 36, 273-293.

Mehta, M.A., Goodyer, I.M., & Sahakian, B.J. (2004). Methylphenidate improves working memory and set-shifting in AD/HD: relationships to baseline memory capacity. *Journal of Child Psychology and Psychiatry,* 45, 293-305.

Meiran, N., Diamond, G.M., Toder, D., Nemets, B. (2010) Cognitive rigidity in unipolar depression and obsessive compulsive disorder: Examination of task switching, Stroop, working memory updating and post-conflict adaptation. *Psychiatry Research,* Epub ahead of print.

Minear, M. & Shah, P. (2008). Training and transfer effects in task switching.*Memory and Cognition,* 36, 1470-1483.

Newman, L.A., Darling, J., & McGaughy, J. (2008). Atomoxetine reverses attentional deficits produced by noradrenergic deafferentation of medial prefrontal cortex. *Pharmacology (Berlin),* 200, 39-50.

Oades R.D. & Christiansen, H. (2008). Cognitive switching processes in young people with attention-deficit/hyperactivity disorder. *Archives of Clinical Neuropsychology,* 23, 21-32.

Poljac, E., Simon, S., Ringlever, L., Kalcik, D., Groen, W.B., Buitelaar, J.K., & Bekkering, H. (2010). Impaired task switching performance in children with dyslexia but not in children with autism. *Quarterly Journal of Experimental Psychology (Colchester),* 63, 401-416.

Robbins, T.W. (2007). Shifting and stopping: fronto-striatal substrates, neurochemical modulation and clinical implications. *Philosophical Transactions of the Royal Society of London. Series B, Biological Sciences,* 362, 917-932.

Roberts, M.E., Tchanturia, K., Stahl, D., Southgate, L., & Treasure, J. (2007). A systematic review and meta-analysis of set-shifting ability in eating disorders. *Psychological Medicine,* 37, 1075-1084.

Rubia, K., Halari, R., Cubillo, A., Mohammad, A.M., Scott, S., & Brammer, M. (2010). Disorder-specific inferior prefrontal hypofunction in boys with pure attention-deficit/hyperactivity disorder compared to boys with pure conduct disorder during cognitive flexibility. *Human Brain Mapping,* Epub ahead of print.

Scheres, A., Oosterlaan, J., Geurts, H., Morein-Zamir, S., Meiran, N., Schut, H., Vlasveld, L., & Sergeant, J.A. (2004). Executive functioning in boys with ADHD: primarily an inhibition deficit? *Archives of Clinical Neuropsychology,* 19, 569-594.

Smith, A.B., Taylor, E., Brammer, M., Toone, B., & Rubia, K. (2006). Task-specific hypoactivation in prefrontal and temporoparietal brain regions during motor inhibition and task switching in medication-naive children and adolescents with attention deficit hyperactivity disorder. *American Journal of Psychiatry,* 163, 1044-1051

St Clair-Thompson, H.L. & Gathercole, S.E. (2006). Executive functions and achievements in school: Shifting, updating, inhibition, and working memory. *Quarterly Journal of Experimental Psychology (Colchester),* 59, 745-759.

White, H.A. & Shah, P. (2006). Training attention-switching ability in adults with ADHD. *Journal of Attention Disorders,* 10, 44-53.

Wylie, G.R., Clark, E.A., Butler, P.D., & Javitt, D.C. (2010). Schizophrenia patients show task switching deficits consistent with N-methyl-d-aspartate system dysfunction but not global executive deficits: implications for pathophysiology of executive dysfunction in schizophrenia. *Schizophrenia Bulletin*, 36, 585-594.

Index

www.ingramcontent.com/pod-product-compliance
Lightning Source LLC
Chambersburg PA
CBHW081157270326
41930CB00014B/3185